Helping Hands

*A Handbook for
Volunteers in Prisons
and Jails*

*By Daniel J. Bayse
Certified Family Life Educator*

Dedication

This book is dedicated to the staff of the Alabama Department of Corrections who taught me how to do prison volunteer work and especially Merle R. Friesen, director of treatment; Paul H. Van Wyk, director of the Bullock County Correctional Facility Intermediate Mental Health Unit; and Pamela C. Van Wyk, director of the Special Programs Unit for Sex Offender Treatment, for their continuing trust and encouragement. These professionals have been much more than supervisors during my years of volunteer service, they have become my mentors and friends.

Perry M. Johnson, President
James A. Gondles, Jr., Executive Director
Patricia L. Poupore, Director of Communications and Publications
Elizabeth Watts, Publications Managing Editor
Marianna Nunan, Associate Editor
Jennifer A. Nichols, Production Editor
Ann M. Tontodonato, Desktop and Print Specialist
Ralph Butler, Cover Design

ISBN 0-929310-85-3

Printed in the United States of America by Graphic Communications, Inc., Upper Marlboro, MD.

Contents

Chapter 1: Yesterday's and Today's Crime, Punishment, and Volunteers

Chapter 2: Understanding the Criminal Personality

Chapter 3: Inmates: Our Reason for Volunteering

Chapter 4: Effective Ways to Work with Inmates

Chapter 5: Avoiding the Pitfalls

Foreword

Volunteers are no longer considered a nice-but-not-necessary part of the corrections workforce; they are important and essential elements in effective inmate management and rehabilitation. They often provide valuable services that would not otherwise be offered in today's world of limited resources.

Helping Hands: A Handbook for Volunteers in Prisons and Jails is written for those interested in volunteering their time and expertise. Like regular employees in correctional facilities, volunteers need to be familiar with the various rules and regulations and policies and procedures that govern the operation of correctional institutions. Although every institution is different and volunteers will need to work closely with the staff and administrators of their particular institution, this handbook provides volunteers with useful and basic guidelines on what they can expect as a volunteer and what is expected of them.

Volunteers are special people who are generous with their time and energy. They can be a great resource to corrections if properly trained.

James A. Gondles, Jr.
Executive Director

Acknowledgments

This book was written with the help of many people. Besides the authors of the many books, journal articles, research projects, and volunteer manuals used as resources for this book, there are many others who made special contributions. My appreciation goes to the state and federal officials who responded to my request for information about their volunteer programs.

A substantial debt of gratitude is owed to three Auburn University professors for their guidance and encouragement: John C. Moracco, Ph.D., and Rick J. Short, Ph.D., Department of Counseling and Counseling Psychology, and David M. Shannon, Ph.D., Department of Educational Foundations, Leadership, and Technology.

Appreciation is expressed to the staff of the Alabama Department of Corrections for their many contributions. Paul H. Van Wyk, Ph.D., director of mental health services, and Pamela C. Van Wyk, director of the special programs unit for sex offenders at the Bullock County Correctional Facility, Union Springs, Alabama, spent many hours editing rough drafts, providing valuable insights into the needs of inmates, and giving encouragement.

Merle R. Friesen, Ed.D., director of treatment, Alabama Department of Corrections, and Deputy Warden Ray Russell, Tutwiler Prison for Women, also provided insight and encouragement. Alabama inmates helped by making contributions to the glossary.

Arnold Fagen of Auburn, Alabama, Lorene Adkins, prison volunteer from Fairfield, Alabama, and Jean Jones, Ed.S., bilingual specialist, Birmingham Public Schools, read the rough drafts and provided helpful feedback. Lee County, Alabama, Circuit Court Judge James Gullege provided insight into the court process.

Prem Gupta, Ph.D., provided much needed insight into his research that led to the development of the Cognitive Moral Theory for Changing Criminals.

Nancy Williams, director, Chaplaincy and Volunteer Services, Maryland Division of Correction; Lynn Doggett, volunteer services program coordinator, Arkansas Department of Corrections; and Deputy Warden Nola Cole, Wyoming Women's Center Corrections, went the "second mile" to help make this book complete. Not only did they provide training materials, but they also contributed research time, hours of telephone consultation, detailed personal correspondence about the needs of female inmates and the problems volunteer coordinators face on a regular basis, and even the lecture notes they use to train volunteers.

The following leaders from the religious community were especially generous in providing materials, insight, and advice on the needs of prison ministry: Donald T. Johnson, director of Missions, Tuskegee Lee Baptist Association, Opelika, Alabama; Miree Tolbert, Alabama area director, Prison Fellowship Ministries; Charles Riggs, chaplaincy administrator for the Federal Bureau of Prisons; Herbert Holley, administrator of the Arkansas Department of Corrections; and Joe Williams, director of Chaplaincy, Baptist General Convention of Oklahoma.

The assistance of the Federal Bureau of Prisons was also appreciated, especially that of J. Michael Quinlan, director; Janie Jeffers, chief, National Office of Citizen Participation; and Vince Micone, administrative assistant.

The following individuals provided copies of their state's or agency's volunteer materials: Helen D. McCullogh, assistant director, Office of Community Resources Development, California Department of Corrections; S. D. Kulmacz, director of the Volunteer Services Unit, Connecticut Department of Corrections; Walter B. Ridley, director of the District of Columbia Department of Corrections; Manoucheher Khatibi, Ph.D., director, Youthful Offender Program Office, Florida Department of Corrections; Larry D. Smith, deputy secretary, Louisiana Department of Public Safety and Corrections; Gary Stotts, Kansas' secretary of Corrections; Frank W. Wood, deputy commissioner, Minnesota Department of Corrections; and Ronald G. Limbeck, administrative assistant, Classification and Programs, Nebraska Department of Correctional Services.

Also to be thanked are Mae McClendon, program consultant, Volunteer Services, North Carolina Division of Prisons; Eloy L. Mondragon, secretary of the New Mexico Corrections Department; William L. Schnitzer, acting director, Volunteer Services coordinator, New York Department of Correctional Services; John D. Morgan, north regional administrative assistant, Ohio Department of Rehabilitation and Correction; William F. Yeager, Volunteer Services coordinator, Public and Employee Services,

Oklahoma Department of Corrections; Fr. Michael W. Sprauer, administrator, Religious Services, Oregon Department of Corrections; J. Harvey Bell, Bureau of Inmate Services, Pennsylvania Department of Corrections; Judy Trosvig, Management Services, Texas Department of Criminal Justice; Walter D. Thieszen, chief of Program Services, Division of Adult Institutions, Wisconsin Department of Corrections; Edward W. Murray, director of the Virginia Department of Corrections; and the State of Washington Department of Corrections.

Last, but not least, I wish to express appreciation to Patricia Poupore, director, Communications and Publications, American Correctional Association (ACA), for her faith in my ability and for being understanding when this manuscript took longer to complete than expected. Linda Munday, ACA's assistant director of marketing, is always a source of inspiration.

Daniel J. Bayse, Ed.S., CFLE

Introduction

Correctional facilities need good volunteers. Prisons and jails are bulging at the seams. Although building new and larger facilities to hold more inmates is one way to handle the problem, it is only a temporary fix. Inmates serve their sentences and are released, but many return to prison. To reduce recidivism, inmates need to be rehabilitated while they are locked up. Hiring treatment personnel is only part of the answer; using volunteers can increase the effectiveness of almost all prison and jail programs.

Lowering crime and recidivism rates has always required community involvement. Volunteers giving of themselves can help turn inmates into productive members of society. When the strong give of themselves to help the weaker members of society, society as a whole is strengthened.

Volunteers can often influence inmates in ways correctional employees can't. Inmates frequently think correctional officials are uncaring. Their words are frequently dismissed as "cop talk" or empty words employees are paid to say. Because volunteers aren't paid to be there, it is harder for inmates to dismiss their words as meaningless.

Inmates live with other inmates. Over time, many begin accepting the attitudes, values, and behavior patterns of the more hardened inmates and become career criminals. Volunteers can help stop this process by being positive role models for inmates. Volunteers can prove to inmates that the whole world is not self-centered. By their presence, they show inmates that people in the "free world" do actually care. Even hardened criminals respond to concern and respect.

It takes a special person to work with inmates. Behind the steel bars are murderers, robbers, rapists, drug dealers, child molesters, and people who are guilty of other equally ugly crimes. Effective prison and jail workers see beyond the crime to the basic value of the individual. They believe in an individual's ability to change

1

and realize that a lifetime of dysfunction doesn't change overnight.

This book is designed to help volunteers become team workers. There is no place inside a prison or jail for a "lone ranger." The person who plows the ground or plants the seeds may not be the one who reaps the crop. Each is equally important if the harvest is to be complete. Corrections work is much the same. Even though some jobs have more prestigious titles, each person who works within the system has a vital role. Each is part of the inmate's rehabilitation process.

Prisons and jails need volunteers who will help, not cause problems. Although most volunteers have a genuine desire to help, many cause problems simply because they don't understand the operation of a correctional facility or how the average inmate thinks. This book is designed to help volunteers gain knowledge of inmates and correctional systems. It even has a glossary to help them understand *some* prison slang.

Working in an environment where freedom is restrained is challenging. Working with a system that is sometimes inflexible and with inmates who seem angry at the whole world (including you) is frustrating. But, it can also be rewarding. I can't think of a more rewarding experience than helping inmates abandon their criminal ways and begin working toward becoming worthwhile members of society.

Chapter 1

Yesterday's and Today's Crime, Punishment, and Volunteers

The Beginning of Crime

Crime is as old as mankind itself. In fact, the biblical account of the first couple on earth reveals that they possessed criminal thought patterns.

In this story, Eve met a con-artist with a long record of trying to overthrow the government. This master manipulator skillfully persuaded her to bypass the posted signs, trespass on private property, steal, and eat fruit. She then took some fruit home to her husband. Adam, knowing it was stolen, willingly took the fruit and ate it. They were caught and questioned. Like most criminals, instead of accepting responsibility, they tried to blame someone else. Adam and Eve became the first of many to use the excuse "The devil made me do it." The truth is that this crime, like *all* crimes that are discovered, consisted of four steps:

1. They saw something they wanted, but had no right to have.

2. They declared that neither God nor society had any right to tell them to control their urges.

3. They abused their power and took it.

4. When they did, they earned the penalty prescribed by the law for their crime.

Adam and Eve, like most criminals, didn't think they would be caught, and the penalty they earned was more than they expected. They were the first of many to learn about the lifelong stigma of being a convicted criminal.

Just like today, when crime became part of their lives their entire world changed. Peaceful living was replaced with fear. Work became a pain. Honesty and openness were replaced with lying and secrecy. A marriage made in heaven itself became a continuing power struggle to determine who would rule the family. Both their son and grandson became murderers. Their descendants became the first of many generations to copy family attitudes, values, and behavior patterns.

With each passing generation the chain of criminality has become stronger. Since 1985, according to the Department of Justice's *National Update* (1992), at least one in four American families has been the victim of serious crimes each year. Prison populations have more than doubled in the past ten years. In fact, Department of Justice (May 1992; June 1992) figures show that by mid-1991, a record 1.21 million inmates were housed in U.S. prisons and jails. An additional 2.7 million people were on probation (Greenfeld 1992). It has become so bad that at the end of 1990, one out of every forty-three adults in the United States was under correctional supervision (Jankowski 1992). Prisons and jails are bulging beyond capacity. Unfortunately, there's no relief in sight.

Clearly something has to be done. Volunteers in corrections are an important part of that "something."

Early Attempts to Control Crime

Ancient tribes quickly learned that the selfish and evil actions of a few required them to band together for their own protection. Crimes that affected the community or angered the gods were considered the most serious (e.g., witchcraft, spying, violations of tribal taboos, etc.). The guilty were usually tortured to death. Early forms of punishment included being stoned, being sealed inside bags with poisonous snakes, being fed to wild animals, or being crucified. Those not executed were frequently ostracized and banned from the community.

Originally, crime committed by one individual against another was not considered a community matter. These types of crimes were settled under the doctrine of *lex talionis* ("an eye for an eye and a tooth for a tooth"). The victim, or the victim's family, was responsible for catching and punishing the criminal. When the perpetrator was caught, the victim or a family member inflicted the original injury on the guilty party. Accidents were not excused.

In *The Story of Punishment,* Barnes (1972) says that the literalness of this method was astonishing. For example, a man who killed another while falling out of a tree was himself killed when the victim's relative jumped out of a tree onto him. Retaliatory wounds were matched as closely as possible to the damage done to the victim. For example, a victim who received a two-inch knife wound to the stomach was required to stab the guilty party's stomach and administer a two-inch knife wound.

This system was ineffective. Angry victims frequently demanded much harsher penalties than they were allowed to inflict. Also, many guilty parties did not willingly submit to this process. They would flee or seek protection from their family and friends. This produced feuds between clans that would sometimes last for generations.

There was another problem. People discovered that revenge can be a very painful experience. Most people don't want the responsibility of personally executing a criminal. Most are reluctant to stick someone with a knife, even if he or she had been a victim earlier.

The Evolution of Criminal Justice

In *A History of Corrections,* Schmalleger (1986) shows that people began to look to their leaders for justice. Punishment by revenge was replaced with a system of fines designed to pay the victims for the harm done to them. Those found guilty of inflicting personal injuries paid higher fines than those convicted of property offenses. These fines were used to pay the victims for their losses.

Historian Hibbert (1978) says that by the seventh century, the amount paid in each case was carefully stipulated. Each body part had a specific value. The loss of an eye cost one amount, a toenail a lesser amount. Executions were reserved for those found guilty of serious crimes, such as treason, murder, or sexual perversion.

Deciding who was telling the truth was, and still is, a problem. Early civilizations frequently used torture to decide the truthfulness of testimony and to gain confessions. Superstition held that the gods would either protect the innocent from harm or would produce supernatural healing. Thus, the accused were required to walk through fire, place their hands in boiling water, endure a hot sword on their tongues, or other equally gruesome "tests." If they were not hurt, or if the wound healed quickly, they were considered to be telling the truth. If not, they were considered to be lying and were executed. Confessions given during these tortures were accepted and frequently used as justification to execute the accused.

During the Middle Ages, people began asking twelve reputable neighbors known as "compurgators" to listen to testimony of both sides and make decisions. Barnes (1972) says that the number twelve was selected because of its significance in both the Old and New Testament of the Bible. This system evolved into the present-day trial by jury.

Courts of law came into existence with the establishment of central governments. Law books were written. Kings appointed magistrates and judges to hear cases and render judgments.

In 1100 A.D., England's King Henry I declared all criminal acts violations of the "King's peace." Fines went into the king's treasury to pay for the "damage" done to the kingdom. Victims were no longer paid for their losses. Instead, they became witnesses for the government and bystanders in the whole judicial process. The courts had complete control of all sentencing—from fines to execution.

Courts began trying to understand why criminals choose to break the law. Punishments were designed to be so awful that the criminal, and those watching, would stop committing crimes.

Thus, punishment was inflicted in the form of public hangings, beheadings, dunking chairs, torture chambers, burnings, and other equally gruesome public executions. Also common were public beatings, brandings, and various other forms of mutilation. For example, thieves might have their hand cut off. To make them unattractive, women caught in adultery lost ears and noses. People caught cursing had holes drilled in their tongues. If not executed, rapists were frequently castrated. Requiring people to spend time in the stocks was popular for a time. To add to the offender's shame, the public was invited to pelt offenders with rotten food, rocks, or whatever else they could find. Many died as a result.

Although public torture is no longer allowed, this basic system is still in use today. Only the local, state, or federal government can charge an individual in a criminal case. Victims are witnesses. Only courts can give sentences, and fines are the property of the government. Offenders, when sentenced, are housed in government-operated prisons and jails. And there is still the hope that the sentences imposed will deter crime.

The Evolution of Prisons and Jails

Until about 300 years ago jails were used primarily to hold people until a trial could be arranged. Large prisons were not needed because once the trial was over criminals received their punishment immediately. The death penalty, when given, was usually carried out by the end of the day.

Early reformers suggested that moving offenders into prison colonies would help reduce crime. Some prison colonies were little more than slave camps. Others gave offenders another chance, sending them to remote areas, such as Siberia and Australia. Many were brought to America. Once in America, convicted criminals could earn their freedom by working as servants, for a specified period.

Times changed, and societies grew. People began noticing that punishment designed to humiliate and torture did little to deter crime. Banishment from one community, or even into a prison penal colony, simply moved the problem from one place to another.

In the sixteenth century, European leaders started gathering criminals and placing them in large workhouses. Most had been arrested for vagrancy. To "cure" their laziness, inmates were forced to spend long hours at hard labor. Conditions in these privately run institutions were horrible. Rules were enforced with whips and other harsh punishments. Inmates had to pay for their room and board. Many were forced to remain after their sentences had expired simply because workhouse salaries did not cover imprisonment costs. Forced prison labor became a source of inexpensive merchandise. Prisons made handsome profits selling the products of the inmates' labor.

The 1700s marked a period of reform in both Europe and America. In 1704 Pope Clement XI created the first "training school" for delinquent boys. The Pope felt that doing hard work while learning discipline would produce repentance. This, in turn,

7

would help turn the delinquent into a productive citizen. It worked, and the basic system that he started is still in use today.

In 1773 Belgium created a prison system that provided separate quarters for men, women, and children. Before this, all offenders, including children, were frequently housed in the same rooms. Harsh punishments and profiting from inmates' work were replaced with efforts to rehabilitate them. Volunteers were used to teach them vocational skills.

In 1790 Philadelphia Quakers created penitentiaries—places to do penance for one's crimes. Inmates were placed in solitary cells with nothing but a Bible. The Quakers believed that inmates could be rehabilitated if they were given enough time to reflect on their evil actions. It didn't work; many inmates thus confined went insane.

Quakers in New York tried a different approach. Inmates were housed in dormitory-type rooms segregated by sex and the seriousness of their crimes. Silence was enforced. Inmates spent long hours in hard labor. Those who refused to obey the rules were placed in solitary confinement for short periods of time. Trades were taught. Men learned to become shoe-makers, weavers, tailors, and carpenters. Women learned spinning, washing, and sewing. Volunteers came into the prison each weekend to teach the Bible and moral values. Inmates eagerly awaited the volunteers' arrival because it was their only contact with the outside world. Leaders from around the world came to study and duplicate this process.

The 1800s saw many reforms. Hibbert (1978) says that in 1833 Tennessee began giving inmates time off for good behavior. Vermont began allowing well-behaved inmates to have tobacco, letters, and visitors. In 1842 Georgia began using a system of rewards and punishments. During this time, Massachusetts began allowing education other than religious instruction. Connecticut prisons began an honor system among inmates. With each reform, the penitentiary, with its focus on the rehabilitation of inmates, became a more permanent part of the criminal justice system.

Volunteers Can Make a Difference

In *Elizabeth Fry: Quaker Heroine*, Whitney (1936) describes a cold January morning in 1813 when two women stepped out of their carriage and walked into London's Newgate prison. Their reaction to what they saw started a volunteer-led prison reform movement that is still active today.

Outside, the huge buildings appeared orderly and beautiful. Inside, Elizabeth Fry was greeted with the stench of squalor. Hundreds of women, reduced to the level of animals by the living conditions, pressed their bodies against the bars hoping for attention. The prison had no beds, windows, or heat, few sanitary facilities, and little ventilation. Except for the ones wealthy enough to purchase straw or lucky enough to get a hammock, inmates slept on dirty wooden floors. Adequate clothing was a luxury.

The two volunteers worked diligently to ease some of the suffering before they left. Inmates were comforted, and clothing was provided for naked babies. Sick inmates were given thick bedding of clean, fresh straw.

Fry couldn't get the sights and smells out of her mind. She became obsessed with prison reform. With the help of British nobility, she founded the Society for the Reformation of Prison Discipline. The modern prison volunteer movement had begun. Volunteers had become the unofficial watchdogs of the prison systems.

Other reformers followed. In 1841 John Augustus, a volunteer from Boston, introduced the practice of placing convicted criminals under the supervision of the community instead of prison authorities. Later he became the nation's first probation officer. In the mid-1800s, the Philadelphia Society for Alleviating the Misery of Public Prisons started a program that supervised newly released inmates. This was the beginning of the modern parole system.

By the mid-twentieth century prison systems began replacing volunteer workers with professional counselors, social workers, psychologists, teachers, and chaplains. As a result, in many systems, volunteers were considered unnecessary and were no longer welcomed within the gates.

Today, prison officials have rediscovered what the Quakers learned two centuries ago. Volunteers are more than simply a way to stretch budgets. Inmates need role models from the free world if they are going to make it on the outside when released. Correctional officials can't provide that role model because they are part of the system.

Today's Criminal Justice System

A criminal's road to jail and/or prison begins when a crime is committed. Frequently, charges are placed when a citizen swears out a warrant. If the crime is witnessed by the police, the criminal may be arrested on the spot. If not, the police will conduct an investigation before placing charges.

In any case, charges cannot be filed without probable cause. Probable cause is the amount of evidence required to convince an ordinary person that the suspect is *probably* the one who broke the law. Once the charges are placed, the case can move into a court of law.

Usually, things that are against the law in one state are against the law in other states. However, because violations are against the "peace and dignity" of the federal, state, or local government, the wording of the laws is created by each governing body. Consequently, the same crime may be called different names in different states. The same crime may also be considered more serious in one state than in another.

Laws that include prison or jail sentences are usually divided into two broad categories: misdemeanors and felonies. These categories determine the maximum sentences that can be imposed for the crime. They also determine the type of court procedure that will be used during the trial. Both categories leave offenders with criminal records.

Misdemeanors

Misdemeanors are less serious than felonies. Examples of misdemeanors could include shoplifting a candy bar, slapping someone with one's hand, or having a small amount of some illegal drugs. If convicted, the maximum penalty for a misdemeanor is spending time in the local jail and/or paying a fine. The limits are set by the state legislatures. Many states set the limit at a $1,000 fine and a year in jail.

Misdemeanors are usually tried in a local court by a judge. These courts may be called the district, city, police, or county court. The trials are usually somewhat informal. There may or may not be attorneys present. Frequently, the people involved in the trial stand in front of the judge to testify. Once the evidence is heard, the judge renders a verdict. If found guilty, the accused has the right to appeal the case to a higher court.

Felonies

Examples of felonies include murder, rape, robbery, and selling drugs. Those convicted of felonies may receive very heavy fines and/or many years in a state or federal penitentiary. "Capital" felonies, such as capital murder, are those crimes that carry the death penalty. Because the penalties are so severe, the law requires that additional steps be taken before a person can be tried, convicted, and sentenced.

After the accused is arrested, he or she is taken to the local jail, where fingerprints and photographs are taken. A magistrate or judge determines (1) if the accused can be released on bond until the trial and (2) if he or she needs to have an attorney appointed to represent him or her during the court proceedings.

Some states require the accused to appear at a preliminary hearing. The preliminary hearing is not a trial; it is a quick review of the evidence by a district or local judge to see if there is enough "probable cause" to support the charge. If so, the charges proceed to the next step. Usually, this is either to the grand jury or, in some states, to trial.

Hearings before grand juries are designed to determine if there is enough evidence to support the charges. Since they do not determine guilt, the accused usually does not testify and is not usually present. Some prosecutions begin at this stage. In this case formal charges would be filed after the grand jury delivers an indictment against the accused.

The actual trial comes next. Although the name of the court varies among states, it is usually called the Circuit Court, Superior Court, or Court of Common Pleas. In New York it is called the Supreme Court. Here the defendant has three choices: (1) plead guilty, or no contest, and hope for mercy, (2) plea bargain for the best sentence possible, or (3) plead "not guilty" and take his or her chances before the judge and/or jury.

A plea of not guilty is not considered a lie, even if the defendant is, in fact, guilty. It simply means that the defendant wants the case to be tried. Normally, a jury hears the evidence. At the trial, each side presents its evidence and a determination of guilt is made.

A finding of guilty does not mean that the evidence was 100 percent conclusive. It only means that the evidence was strong enough for the jury and/or judge to believe "beyond a reasonable doubt" that the accused actually committed the crime.

A finding of not guilty does not mean the person is not guilty. Since, legally, people are innocent until proven guilty, it may mean that the prosecution failed to prove its case. It could also mean that the defense created enough doubt that a guilty verdict could not be supported.

If found not guilty, the accused goes free. He or she cannot be tried again on the same charge in the same jurisdiction, even if additional evidence is found later. If found guilty, a sentence is imposed. Any conviction carries with it the right to appeal the case to a higher court. Sometimes, even the U.S. Supreme Court will agree to hear the appeal. An appeal can be a long and drawn-out process that takes many years.

Appellate courts never declare convicted offenders not guilty. Instead, they determine if the guilty verdict should be overturned because the evidence didn't support the verdict or for some procedural error during the trial. If overturned, the case would go back to the trial court. Sometimes only the sentence is reconsidered. Other times the appeals court may order a new trial. If the prosecutor decides not to retry the case, the defendant goes free.

This is not a perfect system, and mistakes do happen. However, the system is designed to set a guilty person free rather than convict an innocent person. These safeguards make it rare for an innocent person to be convicted and sent to prison.

The Difference between Jails and Prisons

Jails in most jurisdictions are operated by the local sheriff and his or her staff. Since jails are criminals' first stop, cells must accommodate everyone from drunks to mass murderers, and security must be tight.

Jails come in many different sizes and shapes. Justice Department (1992) figures show that 80 percent of the nation's 4,000 jails hold fewer than 50 inmates. Others are large facilities that house more than 3,000 inmates. Treatment facilities range from none to complete rehabilitation and educational staffing.

Unlike in prisons, many inmates in jail have never been convicted of a crime. Many are accused of crimes and are waiting to be released on bond. Others, unable to post bond, are waiting for their trial dates. Some have been found guilty, but are awaiting sentencing. Other inmates may be convicted felons waiting for transfer to a state prison, which can take months. Still others have been convicted of a misdemeanor and are serving their sentences, which can range from a few hours to months.

Being held in jail is very unsettling. So is waiting to be

transferred to prison. Suicide attempts are common. Moods range from remorse and repentance to anger and hostility. Inmates usually don't stay in jail very long. By necessity, volunteer activities must be geared to this reality. However, the kindness of a single volunteer to a jail inmate can bear fruit for years to come.

State Prison Systems

Prisons hold convicted felons. Most prisons are located in remote areas that are not served by public transportation. Each is part of a unified system operated under the authority of an agency usually known as the Department of Corrections. They function with a strict chain of command. Depending on the state, the head is known as the commissioner, director, or secretary. He or she will have a variety of assistants who direct different parts of the prison system. Most states have a volunteer coordinator to direct the activities of the volunteers within the system.

Each prison has a warden or superintendent who is in charge of its overall operation. Both inmates and staff answer to the warden or superintendent. Next in the line of command is the deputy warden, assistant warden, or assistant superintendent. Next are uniformed security staff and civilian employees.

Security staff (known as correctional officers, not guards) form the backbone of the prison. They are responsible for maintaining law and order within the system. Volunteers should work with them and treat them with respect. Inmates watch volunteers closely to see how much they respect staff authority.

Civilian employees make up the rest of the staff. These include people who work in administration, treatment, classification, mental health, health care, education, workshops, maintenance, food services, and the chapel. A volunteer's supervisor is usually one of these people.

The Federal Prison System

The Federal Bureau of Prisons (BOP) was established in 1930 by Congress. It is responsible for the safekeeping, care, protection, instruction, and discipline of all persons charged or convicted of offenses against the United States. To carry out its responsibilities, the BOP has established sixty-seven correctional institutions ranging from penitentiaries to prison camps.

Instead of jails, the BOP has five Metropolitan Correctional Centers. They are designed for offenders serving short sentences or awaiting trial or sentencing. Inmates who require medical, surgical, or psychiatric care may be sent to one of three Federal Medical Centers.

Like state prisons, each federal prison is headed by a warden. The warden is responsible for the safe, secure, and smooth operation of the institution. The chain of command in the federal system is similar to that of most state prison systems.

Names and Titles

People in prisons and jails have names and titles. One of the most important things a volunteer can do to be accepted is to use these titles when addressing personnel. Not only does it show respect, but it graphically demonstrates that the volunteer wants to be part of the system.

Volunteers will have the most contact with correctional officers. They *are not* guards and may be highly insulted if referred to as such. Today's correctional officers are trained professionals who are considered part of the team. It is a stressful job. They have to listen to inmates complain eight hours a day. Inmates resent them. One of the correctional officer's primary responsibilities is helping inmates learn that breaking rules is asking for the penalty that follows. This is a skill inmates must learn if they are to make it on the outside once released.

The proper way to address a correctional officer is "officer" followed by his or her last name. Some jails use the title "deputy." Others simply call the officer by his or her last name. Uniformed supervisors are called by their title (e.g., Sergeant Smith, Lieutenant Jones, or Captain Doe). The uniforms have different insignia that designate different ranks. Volunteers should learn to recognize them and show their respect by calling staff by their proper title.

Each correctional facility is different. Most tend to be formal and call people by their title or use Mr. or Ms. before their last names. Medical doctors and those with doctorate degrees are known as "doctor." Many institutions discourage staff from calling inmates by their first name. If in doubt about what titles to use, volunteers should ask their supervisor what the policy is at that particular institution. It's better to ask than be embarrassed later.

Classification in Prisons and Jails

One way correctional officials try to manage inmates is by classifying them. The most dangerous criminals are placed in maximum security. They usually have long sentences and/or a history of violence. Movement within maximum security institutions is often restricted and monitored closely by security staff. Walls and fences inside the prison keep inmates apart. Activities are usually limited to small groups. These prisons have strict rules.

Medium security prisons house inmates who can usually abide by the rules, as long as they stay inside the prison. The security around the outside edge of the prison complex is very tight. Inside, inmates may have some freedom of movement.

Inmates with low risk factors are housed in minimum security prisons, work release programs, and community-based centers.

Security First, Programs Second

Correctional facilities' primary responsibility is to maintain security. A secondary function is to help inmates successfully reenter family life and society on release.

Prisons are harsh places. About 60 percent of the 1991 prison population consisted of violent offenders or people who had a prior history for violent crimes (Greenfeld 1992). Living in this harsh environment has an effect on inmates. Some will respond with hostility toward staff or other inmates, fear, or even emotional withdrawal. Others use manipulation and con games to get their own way.

Volunteers entering prison or jail for the first time are frequently surprised by the friendliness of inmates. Although many are very nice, looks *can* be deceiving. Many inmates wear their "Sunday manners" around volunteers. Underneath the friendly smile can also be a dangerous con-artist who can fool even seasoned professionals.

Security concerns may require programs to be cancelled at a moment's notice. Sometimes the reason can't be explained. Other times, when tension builds inside the facility, inmates are locked in their cells long enough to cool down. Other times, inmates are "locked down" while staff conduct a search. While frustrating for the volunteer, it is important to remember that this is simply a part of working inside a prison or jail.

Security Includes Screening Volunteers

Because of the security risks involved, volunteers are screened to ensure their compatibility with work in correctional settings. Many states require prospective long-term volunteers to complete written applications. Fingerprints and photographs may be taken. Criminal histories will be checked. All the information obtained is kept confidential and may be used only to decide if the application should be approved.

Volunteer labor is of no value unless it helps the system. Unfortunately, people sometimes exaggerate their qualifications. Volunteers should expect to provide copies of their credentials (e.g., state licenses, diplomas, or certificates). When approved, many states issue volunteers identification cards that allow them entrance into a specific prison. Being a volunteer is a privilege. Breaking the rules can end that privilege.

Being a convicted criminal does not automatically exclude one from being a volunteer. Successful reentry into the free world gives valuable experience that can help inmates. Volunteers who have criminal records should ask the volunteer coordinator to explain prison or jail regulations.

Even one-time volunteers, such as members of church choirs, guest speakers, and holiday project workers are usually screened. Frequently, the names, addresses, dates of birth, and social security numbers of all participants must be furnished to prison authorities at least one week in advance. Prison officials use this information to conduct computerized criminal history checks. This requirement sometimes frustrates long-term volunteers who wish to bring helpers with them.

Prison officials learn from their mistakes. In one instance, a local pastor, who regularly brought church members to worship with inmates, allowed a woman who said she was from another church to join the group at the last moment. The pastor did not know she was wearing two dresses and a wig. As the group was leaving, she left the group on the pretense of going to use the restroom. A few minutes later an inmate left with the group— dressed as a woman. He was found two days later.

Over the years, thousands of people have been caught bringing contraband into prison. For this reason, *everyone* entering a prison or jail is subject to being searched. Many prisons search people at random. Although being searched can be embarrassing, accept it gracefully. It is necessary to make working inside the prison as safe as possible.

Becoming Part of the System

Volunteers are *invited* into prisons and jails to provide specific services. In doing so, volunteers *must not* interfere with the custodial responsibilities of administrators and security staff. Activities must be scheduled in strict accordance with existing institutional routines, rules, and regulations. Prisons and jails *do not* need people who create additional problems.

Volunteers should show staff that they are concerned about staff needs. Prisons are rather depressing places to work. Many volunteers make the mistake of thinking only about what they can do for inmates. In doing so, they begin copying the inmate's contempt for officers and other staff. This does not help the inmate, staff, or volunteer. Volunteers who become part of the team and realize that their job is to help staff perform their mission will find themselves earning the respect of both inmates and staff.

Chapter 2

Understanding the Criminal Personality

Knowledge Prevents Disaster

Working inside a prison or jail without understanding the criminal personality invites disaster. Volunteers can't help inmates change until they understand with whom they are dealing, and even then, only some inmates will change.

Research Helps Us Understand Inmates

Much of what is known about the criminal personality comes from the work of Samuel Yochelson and Stanton Samenow. Their research and published works have identified more than fifty thinking errors displayed by criminal offenders and have become a foundation of many successful prison and jail programs (Yochelson & Samenow 1976, 1977, 1986; Samenow 1984). Prison psychologists Prem Gupta, Gad Czudner, and Ruth Mueller have duplicated many of Yochelson and Samenow's findings (Gupta 1984; Gupta & Mueller 1984; Czudner et al. 1984). This chapter presents a summary of the work by these pioneer prison professionals.

Research usually does not describe specific individuals. Instead, it provides descriptions of the average person in the group that was observed. Accordingly, the majority of criminals can be expected to display most of the characteristics discussed in this chapter. Likewise, some will exhibit all of these attributes, and others may not display any of them at all.

Having these traits does not make one a criminal. Becoming a criminal is a personal choice. Criminals are people who are thinking about, planning, or doing criminal acts. Teaching inmates the aspects of the criminal personality can be an effective way to help them change. It can help them see themselves as they really are.

The Criminal Mask

Masks are useful defense mechanisms. They allow people to continue working even when they feel their entire world is falling apart. Everyone wears them occasionally. However, most people know when to put their masks on and when to take them off. Although their private lives may remain private, "normal" people have nothing to hide. Since their actions match their perception of themselves, they allow people to see who they really are.

Criminals are different. They *do* have things to hide. Thus, they wear a mask all the time. Like chameleons, they quickly change masks so as to match their perception of the environment. For example, an inmate may show remorse or guilt while talking with a volunteer or the parole board but may brag about his conquests to a group of inmates. One mask makes the inmate appear full of religious zeal, another allows this same inmate to "curse like a sailor" in another setting. Many inmates learn to wear masks of responsibility, loyalty, and trust. Since most don't want to serve their entire sentence, they need these masks to convince people they have really changed. Criminals change their masks to suit different audiences.

There's a problem with masks. Nobody knows what the person wearing it is really like. Unfortunately, the average criminal feels too vulnerable to reveal his or her true self.

A Narcissistic Outlook on Life

Research shows that narcissism, or self-centeredness, is the central theme of the criminal's psychological makeup. Life, friendships, and even love are viewed with the thought of what he or she can get out of it. They are always asking, "What's in it for me?" Giving of themselves to help others is a foreign idea.

Self-centered people confuse need, desire, and control in a relationship with love. Some feel that narcissistic people are incapable of love. Gupta and associates suggest that criminals love themselves so much there isn't room to love anyone else.

The American Psychiatric Association's *Diagnostic and Statistical Manual of Mental Disorders* (1987) defines a person with a narcissistic personality disorder as one who has at least five of the following qualities: (1) displays extreme reactions to criticism, (2) is exploitative, (3) feels "special" without appropriate achievement, (4) has unique problems understandable only by other special people, (5) is preoccupied with self-fulfilling fantasies, (6) feels over-entitled, (7) requires constant attention and admiration, (8) lacks empathy, and (9) is preoccupied with feelings of envy. Research shows that the average criminal displays all nine of these characteristics.

The criminal's self-centered nature prevents him or her from showing consideration for others. Altruism, generosity, gratitude, honesty, integrity, modesty, and tact are uncharacteristic of their way of thinking. They usually do not get along well with others.

Narcissistic people frequently strut around like the only rooster in a hen house. Their words and actions say, "I'm number one! I can do anything I want. Say anything I want. Anytime I want. Anywhere I want. To anyone I want! And, there's nothing anyone can do about it."

A Need for Power and Control

The average criminal is motivated by a need to be in power and to control the situation. According to Samenow (1984), criminals consider others their pawns. People are of value only if they bend to the criminal's will. The criminal attempts to accomplish this by force, intimidation, or manipulation.

Prison psychologist Czudner (1985) says that criminals often blame their activity on alcohol, drugs, the company they keep, lack of love or too much love when growing up, poor economic conditions, unemployment, or a host of other excuses. The truth is that criminals do their crimes because they want to do them and enjoy them while they are committing them. However, criminals don't enjoy getting caught.

They crave the excitement that comes with having the power to make victims yield to their demands. Creating and living by their own laws make them feel even more in control. For example, drug dealers enjoy the power of having people beg for their product. Thieves and robbers enjoy forcing people to give them their property. Sex offenders enjoy the self-proclaimed power to pick any man, woman, or child and force them to have sex with them. Murders enjoy the power of having control over life itself.

Many criminals act on impulse. They enjoy the power of not having to control their urges. To the average criminal, "might makes right." Being in control becomes more important than the relationship itself. Even sex is motivated by power and control. It becomes a way to boost the criminal's ego.

This need for power and control doesn't stop when criminals go to jail or prison. The typical criminal tries to dominate every situation and will resort to any tactic to get his or her own way. The most obvious form of this is when criminals simply refuse to obey institutional rules.

Manipulation is a form of overpowering. An inmate may appear to be genuinely remorseful, but in the same breath, the inmate will ask the volunteer to break a "small" rule to help him or her. If this doesn't work, inmates may try angry outbursts or constant pleading until they get their way. Other inmates resort to tears.

Another way of controlling is refusing to listen to another point of view. Compromise is out of the question. Frequently, inmates will pretend to be helpless so someone else will do their assignments.

Criminals have the power to change. Changing means they have to give up their self-proclaimed power and live by society's rules. Many inmates are unwilling to pay that price.

A Lifestyle of Lying

Most people lie occasionally. To some, telling a "white lie" may be preferable to telling a friend that his or her cooking is terrible. To a criminal, lying is a way of life. It feeds the criminal's basic patterns. Yochelson and Samenow (1976, 1977, 1986) claim that to choose to be in crime requires one to lie for self-preservation.

Some people feel that lying can become such a habit that it becomes compulsive. Yochelson and Samenow disagree. Their studies indicate that criminals can readily distinguish between the truth and a lie. They are ready to tell either depending on which will do them the most good. Criminals can become such good actors that they can lie while looking you straight in the eye. Many of them tell the lies so long that they actually start believing them.

Even when criminals tell the truth it is frequently some form of con game. Criminals tell enough truth to gain the listener's trust, then they start lying. They sometimes tell half-truths, thus convincing themselves that they are, indeed, honest. They forget that distortions or anything less than the whole truth is a lie.

Lying is a way to get out of trouble. Many criminals will enlist others to help them lie. Some years ago, a man broke into a warehouse. During the investigation the police found several of his fingerprints. In court, he and his family swore that they were out of the state when the crime happened and that he had never been near that warehouse.

One sex offender set up a camcorder to record his crime. The video was found. He still insists that it is not him on the tape.

Deep inside, criminals think of themselves as good people. To prove this, they will point out how good they are to their family. For example, incest perpetrators will constantly describe how good a parent they were to their victims.

Criminals' lies are often their downfall. Living one's life telling half-truths requires a good memory. It requires remembering which half of the truth was told to whom. Fortunately for the authorities, most criminals aren't as good at remembering as they are at lying.

Antisocial Behavior and Lack of Responsibility

Antisocial behavior is how the criminal personality is expressed. Their deeds fail to conform to society's norms. They repeatedly do deeds that are grounds for arrest, including cheating, stealing, vandalism, physical cruelty, harassing others, or having an illegal occupation. Antisocial people tend to be irritable and aggressive. They're also known to repeatedly get into fights and to commit assaults, including spouse and child beating.

Antisocial individuals have little regard for the personal safety of others. Reckless driving, driving under the influence, and repeated abuse of alcohol and other drugs are common. Sexual promiscuity is the norm. They have few genuine friends.

Early in life, antisocial people begin feeling that they are "different" from everyone else. As a result, many decide to go it alone. This isolation from others prevents them from learning that many others share their same concerns.

Responsibility is understanding one's obligations. This includes one's duty to family and society as a whole. Most criminals like the idea of having children. It boosts their ego. However, some men, in particular, feel no obligation to provide for their family's support.

As a group, antisocial people appear unable or unwilling to keep a steady job. They don't keep appointments, and they have difficulty keeping promises. In classroom settings, they forget the rules of classes or fail to do homework assignments.

Criminals' lack of responsibility keeps them from succeeding in life. Many can sit for hours and talk about the big dreams they hope to achieve when released. Yet, few ever follow through by doing the tasks necessary to achieve those dreams. Instead, they are always looking for a shortcut to fame and financial freedom.

Normal people understand that breaking the law brings with it an expectation of punishment. Criminals will avoid responsibility by trying to make it appear that someone, or something else, *made* them do their crime. Many blame their victim or society. Others blame drugs. Some wear the tattoo "born to lose." This makes fate responsible for their actions.

Low Frustration Tolerance

"I want what I want when I want it" could be the theme song for most criminals. Like a two-year-old child, when they want something they want it now. When criminals' wishes are blocked or delayed, they immediately become angry. This aspect of the criminal mentality prevents them from completing tasks that require sustained effort. When the "going gets tough" he or she gets going—out the door.

According to Samenow (1984), many criminals are remarkably talented. Prisons are full of talented artists who have had little formal training. It's (usually) a joy to listen to inmates sing or play musical instruments they've learned to play by ear. Some are excellent craftsmen. The quality of the leatherwork, furniture, and children's handmade toys can be excellent.

One of the sad aspects of working in a jail or prison is seeing raw talent going to waste. It is even sadder to see inmates take little interest in training and apprenticeship programs. These take perseverance, and most inmates want instant success.

Some inmates lose interest because they aren't disciplined enough to take advantage of the opportunity. Others are so afraid of failure that they give up without trying. The criminal is likely to be turned off by the process of learning. Many feel that it is foolish to learn to do hard work when it's easier for them to gain instant gratification (and money) through crime.

This is frustrating to prison and jail workers. In many cases, volunteers will see inmates take the first steps toward positive change, then suddenly quit. Many will attempt to blame the instructor, counselor, or the staff for making it difficult for them to participate. In most cases, that's not true. The criminal simply hasn't acquired the skills to handle the frustration of completing assignments.

Distorted Ideas about Love

Criminals can be charming, talented, and bright. They can display affection and appreciation. Usually this is a mask. When a criminal talks about love, he or she is usually thinking about what love can do for him or her. Doing something to make the love reciprocal is a new idea to most criminals. As a group, criminals frequently use and manipulate people they love for their own objectives.

For example, most inmates claim to love their mothers. After all, she's the one who has continued to believe in him or her. She's probably been the source of bail money, and she may have paid the attorney. She always accepts the collect phone calls. She's also likely to be rearing the inmate's children. And, in spite of how poorly the criminal may have treated her, she has never given up hope. This is the inmate's kind of love. Inmates have a hard time understanding that receiving love is not the same as loving someone.

Mature love is giving a part of yourself that is the best you have to offer, asking nothing in return but that the gift be accepted. It is never given for selfish reasons, never for personal gain. It is the acceptance and exchanging of gifts of love that causes the relationship to grow.

Inmates, especially men, have a difficult time showing love. Prisons are filled with narcissistic people who look out for "number one." Many are afraid because they equate love with sex. The average inmate feels that displaying kindness and respect are signs of weakness. As a result, caring people become targets fo manipulation. This fear prevents them from changing their distorted ideas about love.

Violence and Anger

Although many inmates wear a mask of calm and control, it usually covers a raging anger that lies just below the surface and frequently erupts into fights and angry words. This anger may appear to be out of control, but it's not. For example, most "spontaneous" fights stop instantly if the warden appears. Instead, its use depends on the criminal's perception of the situation he or she is dealing with.

Violence and anger are also useful to invoke fear or to intimidate others. Other times it is used to cover fear or to create a tough appearance. Violence and anger can even emerge as depression designed to evoke feelings of pity. Regardless of the form, it is being displayed in an attempt to force others into giving the criminal his or her own way.

Lack of Remorse and Guilt

Criminals often confuse guilt with being caught. In a study (Bayse 1989) of a randomly selected group of Alabama inmates, one of the questions inmates were asked started with the words: "Whenever anyone has violated the law, even if he is never charged . . .". At pretest, 58 percent circled the incorrect answer: "he is *in fact* innocent of that crime until proven guilty." Some inmates hold firmly to the belief that they do not *actually* become guilty until a court says they are guilty. Others have insisted that they would *in fact* become innocent if the conviction was overturned by an appeals court. Many inmates find it hard to believe that, convicted or not, criminals become guilty the moment they commit a crime.

Guilt can be a healthy emotion. In *Emotions, Can You Trust Them?*, Dobson (1980) says that appropriate guilt is a message from your conscience that says: "You should be ashamed for what you've done." Guilt should be a guide for moral action. However, to enjoy the fruits of their crimes, criminals must suppress these guilty feelings. Instead, feelings of appropriate guilt are

ιe uneasy feeling that comes with the fear of being

rs, inmates have created innovative ways to con-
s of their innocence. According to Harris (1991),
rationalizations usually fall into distinctive
categories. Many will simply deny their guilt in spite of over-
whelming evidence. One inmate who was photographed by the
bank's security camera while cashing a forged, stolen check still
denied his guilt. His fingerprints were found on the check, and
the forged signature matched his handwriting. He claimed that he
was in another state and someone who looked like him stole his
drivers license and used it for identification.

Others will blame the victim. One inmate, serving a life sentence for killing a state trooper, claimed that if the trooper hadn't
pulled his gun when he reached for his, he wouldn't have *had* to
kill the trooper. Sex offenders often claim that the way the victim
was (un)dressed *caused* the crime.

Others find fault with the system. I'm reminded of a cartoon
showing an inmate talking to a correctional officer. "I want to see
the warden," the inmate says. To which the correctional officer
replied, "Let me guess, you are totally innocent of the made-up
charges that put you here. The judge was crooked, and the police
officers and witnesses lied on the witness stand. And, besides
that, your attorney did not represent you properly." "Hey," the inmate exclaimed, "I see that you've already heard about my case!"

Others feel they were entitled to commit their crimes because
of some past injustice. For example, many claim that perceived
improper action by the police entitles mobs to riot, loot, and ter-
rorize neighborhoods. Many inmates attempt to justify their actions with words like, "I did what anyone would do in a situation
like that." Some years ago in Richmond, Virginia, a man was
charged with killing his wife. He had found her in bed with
another man. In court, the judge asked the defendant why he
killed her instead of her lover. He replied, "She was so unfaithful
that if I killed him I would have had to kill another one next
week."

Still others will blame society's ills, their home environment,
or their own insanity as being responsible for their crime. Saying
that alcohol or other drugs "cause" them to do their crime is becoming an increasingly popular defense.

These excuses are designed to make it look like the crime was
not the criminal's fault, making the criminal the victim. Because
of this, many don't see any reason to feel remorseful for their actions.

Lack of Empathy

Criminals, as a group, do not have the ability to empathize: to put themselves in someone else's shoes. This is a skill that is necessary for anyone who desires close interpersonal relationships. Close friends are those who can share each other's pain and joy.

Yochelson and Samenow's (1976, 1977, 1986) research shows that criminals have little concern about the effect of crime on their victims. Frequently, they will deny any harm was done. Common to their thinking are words like: "He wasn't really hurt when I stabbed him. He only spent a few hours in the hospital, and he recovered in a couple of weeks." Or, "What are they so mad about? The insurance company took care of the damages. It didn't cost them anything."

Child molesters frequently say, "I didn't really hurt her (or him). All I did was touch." Rapists frequently use a similar statement, "She didn't really get hurt. After all, I didn't cut her or anything." Many inmates have no concept of the lasting emotional harm that is done when a person is a victim of a crime.

Inmates as a whole do not understand how their actions have hurt their families. For example, my own research (Bayse 1982) has shown that 49 percent of inmates agreed that "anytime you do something in your home that proves you to be untrustworthy it gives the family a chance to practice forgiveness and makes the family stronger."

It is difficult, but inmates can be taught to respect the feelings of others. It is only then that rehabilitation can begin.

Labels Can Be Dangerous

The danger in generalizing about inmates is that some people will assume that all inmates fit this stereotype. This is not the case: inmates are individuals. Although many have common features, all people who work in prisons and jails, including volunteers, should treat each individual inmate with the dignity that he or she deserves.

Chapter 3

Inmates: Our Reason for Volunteering

There is never enough time, unless you're serving it.

Malcom Forbes

Crime: The Great Equalizer

Prisons and jails hold people from all socioeconomic groups, ages, races, and gender. Everyone from former presidential aides to skid-row bums has lived there. Inside, it's not unusual to see a former doctor sleeping next to a former construction worker. Former ministers share cells with former drug dealers, former college professors with the illiterate. Yet, their uniforms tend to make them all look the same.

A majority of inmates feel their crime was caused by unmanageable, powerful, external forces. Most have sad stories to tell. To offer only sympathy reinforces the inmate's idea of being the absolute victim of these external forces.

Inmates have decisions to make, lives to restore. Most genuinely don't want to come back to prison or jail. Only a few have the skills to make that dream come true. Volunteers must work together with staff to help inmates discover, understand, explore, try, and take responsibility for their options. Volunteers must help inmates realize they have the power to change. Only then can inmates begin feeling like capable human beings with the ability to survive in the "free world."

Imprisonment Changes People

Inmates live in an atmosphere of deprivation where each day seems like the one before. Once inside the walls, inmates lose most of their independence and control over their lives. They are stripped of legitimate power and most of their possessions. Their status is that of a social outcast. Separation from families and other meaningful aspects of life leaves many feeling abandoned and desolate.

There are many natural responses to living in this type of environment. Frustration, fear, anger, depression, and feelings of hopelessness are common. Inmates, like all of us, try to adapt to their surroundings. Some of the ways they adapt are healthy. Included in these are seeking counseling, participating in programs, and maintaining contact with families and friends. Others, such as conforming to the inmate code and manipulating people, are not.

Inmates, submerged in their feelings of alienation from society, create their own social standing. Unfortunately, this is based on their accomplishments in crime. At one end are the heros—the murderers, especially cop killers. At the opposite end are the sex offenders—child molesters are considered the lowest of the low.

Inmates live with inmates. Because of this, many inmates become "prisonized" or "institutionalized." This occurs when inmates begin accepting the attitudes, norms, values, and behavior patterns of more hardened criminals. Criminal skills are honed in prisons. Prisonized inmates usually return once released. Today's research shows that an effective preventive measure is for inmates to have continual contact with people from the "free world." This is one of the reasons that having volunteers in correctional facilities is so important. It helps inmates focus on becoming part of their community once again.

Life behind Bars

Prisons are not nice places to live. A common complaint among inmates is the feeling that no one can be trusted. Their every move is watched by correctional officers. Because of this, they live with the feeling we have when there's a police car in our rear view mirror. Many inmates will act friendly just so they can find out things about other inmates. Then, if they think it will be beneficial to them, they will gladly tell prison officials the other inmate's secrets. As a result, many inmates are afraid to make friends.

Inmates always fear being set up for a fall. Many inmates are released on parole. As a means of control, inmates will frequently do things that will hurt another inmate's chances for an early release.

There is little or no privacy. Windows or bars allow constant observation. In many places, inmates aren't even trusted to go to the toilet or shower in private. They are watched because prison officials know that body cavities are a popular way to smuggle drugs or transport them throughout the system. The correctional officer watching may be of either sex. Equal opportunity employment laws require this.

Inmates are subject to search at any time. In some cases these searches require inmates to remove their clothing or allow their body cavities to be examined. This requirement is necessary to keep weapons or other forms of contraband out of the prison.

In *Breaking into Prison*, Buckley (1974) tells of an inmate who had a visitor continually bring in an abundant supply of dental floss. The visitor grew tired of this, but felt sorry for the inmate because the prison did not supply dental floss. One day when the visitor came the inmate was gone. The inmate had used the dental floss to fashion a ladder and escape.

Incoming mail is opened and checked for contraband. Schedules are set. Meals are served at prescribed times. Even the serving trays and utensils are chosen with security in mind.

Griping about the food is a favorite pastime. Part of the loss of power includes the inability to choose when, where, and what one eats.

Inmates quickly discover that their sexuality doesn't stop when they enter prison or jail. There are few, if any, legitimate outlets for sex. This causes a lot of pain. Many fights are caused by the homosexual advances of other inmates. The lack of privacy can make any sexual activity, even masturbation, an embarrassing public affair.

Many inmates blame the system and feel there is little they can do to control their lives. Some regain power by "giving in" and learn to placate those in authority. Others rebel. Conflict is inevitable. Some use the time to learn from their mistakes. These are the ones who can be helped.

Inmates in Jails

The Department of Justice (June 1992) reports that during the year ending 29 June 1990 there were nearly 20 million admissions and releases in the nation's jails. On 30 June 1990, locally operated jails and correctional facilities held a record 405,320 people (Greenfeld 1992). Department of Justice (August 1991) statistics indicate that this figure has increased 77 percent during the past six years. Drug violations were responsible for 40 percent of this increase.

According to the Department of Justice (June 1992), 91 percent of the jail inmates were male and 9 percent were female; 41 percent were white and 43 percent were black. Hispanics accounted for 14 percent of the jail population. On the average, jail inmates spend at least fifteen hours per day in their cells. Only half have work assignments. The most common work assignments are janitorial, maintenance, office, and food service duties (Department of Justice March 1992).

Prison Populations

Department of Justice statistics show that on 30 June 1991 the population in state and federal prisons reached an all-time high of 804,524 inmates (Greenfeld 1992). The Criminal Justice Institute (1990) reports that 487,227 of these were admitted during 1989. About 80 percent of these inmates had either been in prison, in jail, or on probation before beginning their sentence (Greenfeld 1992). Prison populations have more than doubled in the past ten years, with drug and alcohol use playing a major role. Two-thirds of inmates serving time for a violent offense were under the influence of alcohol or other drugs when they did their crime (Department of Justice 1991).

The Criminal Justice Institute (1990) reports that on 1 January 1990 the average prison inmate was 29.6 years old. The racial mixture included 50.9 percent white, 35.7 percent black, 9.6 percent Hispanic, and 3.6 percent Native American. Other races accounted for the remainder.

In *Prisons and Prisoners in the United States* (1992), Greenfeld says that the inmate's average prison sentence was 6.1 years, with approximately 24 percent receiving sentences of 15 years or more. On the average, inmates were released after serving 34 percent of their sentences. At least 123,000 of the 386,228 inmates who were released in 1989 are expected to return within three years (Criminal Justice Institute 1990).

Male Inmates

A study (Bayse 1989) of Alabama medium security inmates revealed that their years of education ranged from 2 to 19, with an average of 11.1 years. Only 19 percent were legally married. However, 48 percent were presently involved in a long-term relationship with a significant other. The remainder were single. A large majority of the inmates (46 percent) were still attached to their legal wives or significant others. Only 18.5 percent divorced between the time of their arrest and present imprisonment. Although 32 percent of the inmates were childless, the remaining 68 percent had produced an average of three children each.

Inmates frequently enter prison with their family relationships in distress and rapidly deteriorating. The inmates in the Alabama study were no exception. Slightly over half were less than happy with their present family relationships. In that study, the more self-centered the inmate, the more disengaged he felt from his family.

Although this research applies only to Alabama inmates, the figures are consistent with current research and with inmate groups in other states. For example, twenty-three inmates who participated in a volunteer-led family life seminar in Oklahoma listed a total of thirty-one marriages and thirty-four "common law relationships." The nineteen inmates who had children listed sixty-four children and twenty-five grandchildren. Most were less than happy with their family relationship.

Male prisons are "macho" places where the strong survive by acting or being tough. Few male inmates have any real plans about what they will do once released, except for some vague plans about the great job they will find. Unless some intervention changes their thinking, most will return to the same "hard living" lifestyle that put them in prison in the first place.

Female Inmates

Female inmates have always been in the minority. In 1990, jail populations were 9.5 percent women. Prisons held 5.6 percent women. Female inmates face many issues that are similar to those faced by men. These include the lack of marketable job skills, the need to eliminate criminal thinking patterns, and the need to learn relationship and/or parenting skills. Both sexes need to learn that they have the power to break the chains that bind them to their past improper actions and establish a new and productive life once released.

Women also face many issues that are different from those faced by men. For example, Department of Justice (March 1992) statistics found that about 44 percent of female inmates *reported* that they had been either physically or sexually assaulted at some point in their lives. Observation by prison professionals suggests that the actual figures are much higher. Women are more likely to have been emotionally close to their victims of violent crimes. In general, female inmates use more drugs and use them more frequently than male inmates.

When a man goes to prison his family usually maintains supportive contact. Not so with women. Riggs and van Baalen (1992) in a small study found that male inmates received twice the number of visits as did female inmates. For women, prison can be an especially lonely place.

Many women enter prison from a single parent role. Others give birth in prison. Less than 25 percent of the fathers are willing to assume custody. Many lose their children to foster care. Female inmates, much more than their male counterparts, grieve the loss of their children and voice their concern about their welfare regularly.

As a group, women aren't afraid to show their emotions and express their feelings. They are more likely to self-disclose in groups. However, most also know how to use their behavior and/or emotions to manipulate others. For example, crying can tug on a volunteer's heartstrings. When this happens, volunteers must make a quick assessment and decision. In some cases, it is important to show comfort and deal with the issue causing the pain. On the other hand, if the crying is an attempt to control, it is important to get on with the agenda of the meeting.

Prison officials in Alabama, Wyoming, Maryland, and the Bureau of Prisons have indicated that unlike male inmates, female inmates have a need to be touched. Although touching is more tolerated in prisons for women, it presents a delicate problem. Sound correctional practices require a professional distance be maintained between inmates and staff, including volunteers. Some women are seductive and will use an "innocent" flirt to start the process. Men, in particular, need to be aware of this. Volunteers should discuss with their supervisors and understand the institution's policy about touching inmates before they begin their duties.

Throughout the ages women have established their identity and found fulfillment by nurturing others, providing for their children, and building secure relationships. As a group, they thrive on intimacy and being connected to special people in their lives. To replace what they had to leave behind, female inmates frequently create pseudofamilies inside prison walls. Like on the outside, these "families" usually have problems. Issues of dominance, jealousy, and physical, sexual, or emotional abuse are common. Many need help as they balance their need for intimacy and relationships with the limits of their own morality. Volunteers must be careful not to allow themselves to become manipulated into assuming a leadership role in one of these "families."

Inmates Are "Cultural" People

Crime knows no cultural barriers. Unfortunately, racial prejudice still exists within prison walls, just as it does on the outside. Discrimination has no place in volunteer service.

Lambert (1991) notes that culture is a learned experience. It is how one generation shares its attitudes, beliefs, values, and behavior patterns with the next generation. One's culture could include languages, foods, traditions, customs, and learning styles.

Respecting an inmate's cultural heritage is showing respect to that individual. Volunteers need to be aware of cultural differences. For example, Cesarez and Madrid-Bustos (1991) say that showing respect to Hispanic men may require reprimanding them one-on-one and away from their peers. Many Native Americans feel that looking someone in the eye shows disrespect.

Many inmates come from impoverished, dysfunctional, minority families. As a result, deep resentments stemming from years of discrimination are common. Because of this many have learned to distrust people of different races. Overcoming this requires volunteers to demonstrate a basic respect for each inmate and his or her culture. However, many inmates use cultural differences as an excuse for breaking the rules and/or their criminal activity. Over the years many volunteers have been manipulated into falling in this trap.

Showing respect to inmates includes understanding the background that helped place them inside the walls. However, understanding their values does not require you to agree with them.

Inmates Live by the Inmate Code

Part of becoming prisonized is learning to live by the "inmate code." Life inside prison is a constant power struggle between the criminal element and the rules of the system. This code allows inmates to create and live by their own rules without fear of punishment. Inmates enforce this code with a vengeance. Violations are met with sanctions ranging from ostracism to physical violence or death, especially in maximum security prisons.

As explained in the training materials used by the Kansas Department of Corrections, there are six chief tenets of the inmate social code:

1. **Be loyal.** There seems to be an unwritten rule throughout prisons that says inmates must be loyal to each other. This includes maintaining a "code of silence" about criminal activities done by other inmates. Inmates are expected to lie if necessary to protect other inmates who they know have violated the rules. This loyalty is demanded regardless of the personal cost to the individual inmate. Inmates are never to take a problem to prison staff. Doing so would be considered a breach of loyalty.

2. **Be cool.** Inmates are to always be in control. They are to refrain from quarrels or arguments with fellow inmates. They are to remain cool regardless of how much pressure they receive from correctional staff. Their slogan seems to be: "Just do your time and don't make waves."

3. **Be straight** *(with your fellow inmates)***.** Don't take advantage of another inmate. Don't lie. Don't break your word. Don't steal. Pay your debts. Inmates should share with one another by exchanging goods for gifts or favors. Unfortunately, many inmates break this rule, causing friction among inmates. Being straight with a staff member is telling enough half-truths to get off or doing what is necessary to get one's way.

4. **Be tough.** Don't weaken, don't whine, and don't cry guilty. The inmate should be able to "take it" without quivering. Although the inmate code discourages

inmates from starting a fight, running from a fight that someone else starts is considered disgraceful.

5. **Be sharp.** Don't be a sucker. Correctional officers are to be treated with suspicion and distrust. Whenever there's a conflict between an officer and an inmate, always assume that the correctional officer was wrong.

6. **Be right.** This is combination of the other five. An inmate is "right" when he or she is loyal to fellow inmates. Inmates can depend on him or her. The right inmate never interferes with another inmate's schemes to break prison rules. He or she doesn't back down if someone picks a fight. Right inmates know their rights and use them to get their way. He or she can take whatever the prison system dishes out and never flinch.

Inmates Are Narcissistic

As explained earlier, narcissism or self-centeredness is the average inmate's most prominent feature. They look out for "number one"—themselves. Narcissistic people concentrate on getting their own needs met. They expect others to give them what they desire without complaint. In fact, putting the needs and feelings of others ahead of their own is a foreign idea to most inmates. It is considered to be a sign of weakness.

Narcissistic people live by their own rules. Since these types of people see kindness as weakness, any display of concern is likely to be met with an attempt to control. Tardiness, constant trips to the toilet, failure to do assignments, or dominating group discussions are the norm. So is simply getting up and leaving.

A consequence of being self-centered is the inability to see how one's actions affect others. As a result, they can't understand how other people feel about what they have done. Yet, these same inmates will protest loudly if another narcissistic inmate insists on having his or her own way.

Inmates Have an External Locus of Control

Social scientist Heider (1958) defined locus of control as a personality variable referring to the feelings of control that individuals *perceive* they have over their lives. Emotionally healthy people have an internal locus of control. They realize their lives are controlled by their ability and/or the amount of effort they expend to complete tasks. People with an internal locus of control feel they have the power to choose their own destinies.

Researchers have known for years that people who feel in control of their lives are usually happier and more successful than those who don't feel in control. People with a strong internal locus of control realize they have the ability to rise above their present situation. This enables them to build better lives for themselves. They learn from their mistakes. What they lack in ability is made up by putting out the extra effort to get the job done. People like this fully understand the meaning of the adage: "You'll never know how much you can do until you've bitten off more than you can chew."

Unhealthy personalities, including criminals, have an external locus of control. They feel that their lives are controlled by luck, the difficulty of the task, or powerful others. Many inmates grew up in homes where they were physically, sexually, or emotionally abused. An external locus of control is easily formed in abusive homes where the child's life is literally controlled by the anger or sobriety of the parent.

Research and common observation demonstrate that inmates have an external locus of control. Consequently, most inmates believe that external forces control their lives. Because of this, they feel powerless to choose their own behavior and/or chart their own destinies. They blame their crimes on external forces. Many honestly believe that someone or something other than themselves caused them to do their crime.

Many Inmates Are Religious People

Religion can be very important to inmates. For some, it becomes an innovative way to meet their own needs. Con-artists have done this for years. In *Breaking into Prison*, Buckley (1974) describes a lawsuit filed by a group of inmates complaining about the lack of religious freedom inside the prison. The suit asked the court to require the prison to recognize their "Church of the New Song" and to require the prison to furnish the materials for its liturgy—steak and wine for all of their followers.

Not all inmates are like that. Lonely cells and cold steel bars have a way of breaking the human spirit. Faith in God provides the promise of forgiveness, healing, restoration, and a new abundant life. Out of their desperation many inmates reach out for that promise. For that reason, religious volunteers find correctional facilities a field "white unto harvest."

Many men and women experience true religious conversions inside prisons and jails. Frequently, religious workers find that changes started in a jail will bear fruit by the time an inmate gets to prison. Many inmates, with time on their hands, spend countless hours doing in-depth Bible studies. Some religious leaders feel that a nationwide, large-scale spiritual awakening may result from these studies. A study funded by Prison Fellowship Ministries found that inmates who participate in religious instruction while incarcerated have lower recidivism rates (Gartner et al. 1990).

Some changes are real and some aren't. According to Prison Fellowship (1989), inmates usually want volunteers to like them. As a result, many inmates will make repeated religious commitments simply to please the volunteers. One chaplain told of asking volunteers to provide the total number of inmates who made religious commitments during their services. At the end of one year, 2,100 inmates in that prison had made *first time* professions of faith in God. The prison only held 700 inmates.

Religious volunteers are frequently surprised to discover that prison officials don't share their excitement. Volunteers only get to see the enthusiasm displayed by inmates during services. Prison officials see the results of "jail house religion." While true religion is a way of life, many narcissistic inmates want the forgiveness and acceptance that religion promises without having to follow the strict moral guidelines that are part of its teaching. It's not unusual for inmates to make a religious commitment and then ask, "Well, I've been forgiven, when do I get to leave?"

Prison officials and chaplains have learned not to take inmates' religious commitments at face value. Instead, they will wait to see if inmates' lives show positive change.

Religious freedom does not stop at the prison doors. Inside the walls are people of all religions. Followers of every faith are convinced that they have found the "One True God." Arguing rarely convinces anyone to change. It solidifies positions. In this case, it may be best to agree to disagree.

Many religious volunteers focus their attention on messages designed to convert inmates to their faith. This may be an appropriate message for a transient population such as a jail. The men and women in prison are long-time residents. They desire the same type of messages they would hear in their churches or synagogues back home. They want to know how to apply spiritual principles to their everyday lives.

Inmates Can Change

Volunteers will frequently hear inmates say: "I just can't do it. It's just too difficult." This sentiment has prevented many inmates from becoming useful and productive members of society. Volunteers by their very presence demonstrate their faith in an inmate's ability to change. Inmates must be led to realize that the word "can't" usually means "won't." Inmates must be helped to realize the potential in their own abilities. Understanding how much their lives would change if they made an effort would empower them with the ability to change their lives.

Chapter 4

Effective Ways to Work with Inmates

I count him braver who overcomes his desires than him who conquers his enemies; for the hardest victory is the victory over self.

Aristotle

Ways Prisons and Jails Use Volunteers

Ways correctional facilities use volunteers are limited only by the imagination. Many minister to the spiritual needs of inmates. Others work in drug treatment programs or programs that follow the twelve-step traditions (e.g., Alcoholics Anonymous, Narcotics Anonymous, Gamblers Anonymous, and Sex Addicts Anonymous). In some states, inmates receive individual, group, and/or family counseling from volunteers. Volunteers are also used for staff assistance, arts and crafts, recreational programs, transportation, and prerelease programs. Others teach GED classes, literacy, high school, vocational education, and even college courses to inmates.

Volunteers have created many innovative programs. For example, volunteers in Connecticut operate a retail outlet that sells items produced by inmates in prison hobby shops. Several states have an "M-2 program," which matches volunteers with inmates for regular monthly visits. Others have helped inmates create chapters of the National Association for the Advancement of Colored People, the Jaycees, and other civic organizations.

Correctional facilities are an excellent source of college practicum and internship placements. Staff members will encourage students to become part of the team. Although these positions are usually unpaid, the experience received is priceless. For example, the Alabama Department of Corrections used a graduate student to create, implement, and research their first family life psychoeducational programs. These programs are now being used by other states.

Starting Your Own Program

Prison systems frequently allow qualified individuals or groups to create their own program. Most require a detailed, written application process, with a multistep approval process. Programs that appeal to a broad range of inmate needs and interests are more likely to be approved than those that don't.

Having a great idea doesn't guarantee acceptance, especially if a similar program already exists. Sometimes good programs are disapproved or cancelled because there isn't enough security coverage available without paying overtime. Even "free" programs cost prison systems money.

Wise volunteers are willing to work with the system. If rejected, they will try to adapt to the needs of that facility or they will try another facility. Some make the mistake of trying to force their programs on prison officials. Prisons, like all places, can be difficult places to work if you're not part of the team.

Look the Part

Volunteers should dress appropriately for the positions they fill. Regulations require that clothing look different from prison uniforms. Don't wear clothing that could be considered seductive. Women shouldn't wear heavy make-up or perfume. Tight, short, low-cut, or transparent clothing will not be allowed. Earrings are prohibited in many places. Don't wear expensive

jewelry or watches. Purses and briefcases should never be left un-
attended. Many facilities require that they be left in the car.

When in doubt, it is best to check it out. Don't be embarrassed
by being turned away from the gate because you wore clothing
considered inappropriate for that facility.

Stages to Effectiveness

Becoming an effective volunteer is not automatic. Arkansas'
Volunteer Manual and Maryland's *Volunteer Pre-Service Training Guide* show that individuals or groups usually go through
three stages after beginning to work in a correctional facility.

Stage One

Most volunteers start by feeling sorry for inmates and relating
to them in a paternalistic or condescending manner. Others expect to be treated like royalty because they are donating their pre-
cious time. Still others remain aloof or detached and treat inmates
as if they were objects instead of people. This type behavior is
destructive to both inmates and volunteers. Volunteers in this
stage may do more harm than good.

Stage Two

During this stage volunteers become angry with the system.
They will openly question the staff's motives, the way programs
are developed, or why particular inmates are still incarcerated.
Volunteers may become impatient with the many rules and
regulations. They may begin to offer simplistic, easy fixes to difficult problems.

A shift usually occurs during this stage. Instead of putting
down inmates, volunteers begin putting down the people who
detain them. Their focus on inmate issues makes them unaware
of their own blind spots. As a result, these volunteers miss
pathological or obvious criminal thinking patterns that make inmates a poor risk for release. Volunteers in this stage generally
do not treat staff with respect. While this behavior may be
popular with inmates, ultimately it is destructive to everyone involved.

Stage Three

During this stage volunteers progress to a more balanced position. They begin looking at people and situations objectively. Issues will be faced in an open and honest manner. They begin learning the strengths and weaknesses in the personnel, programs, and the institution itself.

Volunteers in this stage begin to see things realistically. They begin discovering how inmates, staff, and volunteers can complement one another. This allows the rehabilitation process to become a collaborative effort. First impressions and over-generalizations regarding all staff and all inmates are dropped. In its place comes an understanding of the adage: "You can't see eye to eye with others until you quit looking down on them."

Once volunteers reach this stage, they can attend effectively to the needs of those they serve. They are useful because they have become a valuable part of the team.

Qualities of a Good Volunteer

Adults of all ages, all educational levels, and from all walks of life can become good volunteers. Correctional systems need level-headed people who are willing to share their experience or training with inmates and want to be part of the team. Effective volunteers also tend to have the following qualities.

Be Ethical

Every professional organization has ethical standards that guide the practice. ACA's are provided on the inside back cover of this book. However, being ethical is more than simply following a set of rules, it is a way of life.

Ethical living means treating others with respect, no matter how they treat you. It's treating others the way you want to be treated. Ethical living is having nothing to hide. It's not caring who watches you or worrying about being seen in the "wrong place." It's doing what is right simply because it's the right thing to do.

Be a Good Listener

Everybody needs someone who will listen to him or her. Inmates are no exception. They experience joy, sorrow, happiness, and sadness just like everyone else. They need someone who cares about their thoughts and feelings. Listening to what inmates say makes their words valuable, enhancing their self-esteem.

Inmates will be cautious at first. Most have never had anyone who really listened to their needs. However, as inmates learn that you are trustworthy, they will begin opening up. Listen for themes in the conversation. What they repeat is probably what is bothering them.

Be Empathic, but Not Gullible

Empathy is showing others that you are willing to look at life from their perspective. It also involves communicating that understanding to him or her. Volunteers can't be effective until they have an understanding of the pressures, needs, interests, capabilities, and limitations of inmates from the inmate's point of view.

However, empathy does not require you to abandon your beliefs, values, or feelings. Nor does it mean that you must agree with the inmates' position. Instead, it is listening with the intent to understand. It does not mean believing everything you hear. Some volunteers overidentify and begin feeling *like* the inmates. This brings the volunteer down to their level and makes it harder for them to help.

Be Respectful

To be effective, volunteers must simultaneously respect inmates as individuals, empathize with their pain, and believe in their capacity to change. There is no room for prejudices or feelings of superiority in a prison setting.

Will Rogers said: "I never met a man I didn't like." Most of us are less tolerant. The words "love the sinner but hate the sin" are easy to say. However, as Salter (1988) says, it is difficult to extend respect to people who frequently lie, con, deny, and minimize behavior that is harmful to others.

Sometimes, showing respect is being honest enough to withdraw. Occasionally, there may be inmates you simply can't deal with because of their personality or crime. If this happens, talk it over with your supervisor. Admit that it is your problem and not the inmate's. Sometimes it can turn the tide.

Let the relationship grow. Inmates, like others, require you to earn their respect and trust before they will open up. Respect is responding to the inmate's interests and needs instead of your own.

Don't pry. Let inmates decide when to reveal details about their crime, their past, or other concerns. Think about it: do you enjoy people asking about your past just to satisfy their own curiosity?

Be Genuine

Being genuine is allowing people to see the real you. It involves expressing your true feelings with tact and consideration. It's being "straight" and talking without using words that have double meanings.

Genuine people can even take criticism without becoming defensive. They know themselves, including their strengths and weaknesses. When someone expresses a negative opinion about them, instead of getting hateful, they will try to understand the other person's point of view. Genuine people are honest and will share their feelings if someone else's behavior makes them uncomfortable.

How can one become genuine? As Oklahoma's *Handbook for Citizen Involvement in Corrections* says, "Be your 'best' self, but be yourself." Inmates can usually spot a phony a mile away.

Be Patient

There are many sources of frustration in correctional facilities. Sometimes frustration can take root while waiting for the outside gates to open, especially if it's cold or raining. Prison schedules are subject to change at a moment's notice. Security takes first priority. A fight, a missing key, the suspicion that an inmate is missing, or another unexplained reason could cause the entire facility to be "locked down." When this happens, all inmates are returned to their cells. This could last for minutes, hours, or even days.

It's not unusual to arrive and find that the room needed for the program is not set up. Frequently, prisons don't allow inmates to leave their cellblocks until the session's scheduled starting time. Communication failures can cause problems. For example, a warden mailed 600 invitations to family members to attend an inmate/family seminar I was to conduct. Somehow the memorandum with the details was not delivered to security staff. When I arrived on Saturday, security staff had no idea I was coming. Fortunately, I was early and had copies of the paperwork with me. It prevented a major disaster from happening. Things like this happen. Effective volunteers allow time for the unexpected. Those who roll with the punches will earn the respect of inmates and staff members alike. It also saves a lot of ulcers.

Be Trustworthy

Effective volunteers do not make promises unless they are prepared to carry them out. Inmates will test volunteers, or call their bluff, just to see if they will indeed keep their word. Once you break their trust you've lost them.

Being trustworthy includes telling inmates the limits of confidentiality. Not everything can be kept confidential. For example, not advising staff about a planned escape could result in prosecution in some states. Ask your supervisor about the rules at your facility and be up front with inmates. I make it a policy to keep no secrets from my prison supervisor. Inmates are made aware of this from the beginning; it's up to them to decide what they want to reveal in counseling sessions.

Being trustworthy is showing up on time and following the rules. It also means not allowing inmates to con you into helping them break the rules. Being trustworthy is creating a name for yourself that means dependable and faithful.

Be Confrontive

Confrontation is showing inmates the difference between their statements and their actions. This should be done in a normal tone of voice or even humorously. Hostile confrontation is seldom effective. In *Tough Customers: Counseling Unwilling Clients*, Ganley (1991) says that using confrontation appropriately helps inmates not to rely on minimizing, denying, and blaming their crime on external forces. Appropriate confrontation helps inmates see themselves as they really are. This, in turn, gives them reasons to change their ways.

Most inmates come from dysfunctional backgrounds. Stories they tell may tug on the heartstrings of any caring individual. This makes it easy to create an inappropriate relationship. Effective volunteers realize that a criminal's past may have been a contributing factor in his or her decision to break the law, but it did not *cause* it. Constructive confrontation helps inmates accept responsibility for their behavior.

When confronting inmates, Salter (1988) recommends responses such as "Give me a break! What do you mean one drink can't do any harm?" Or, "Do you really expect me to believe that you broke open the door just to get in out of the cold?" Or, "I can't promise that I will always agree with you, and I don't expect you to always agree with me. I can promise, however, to always be straight with you, and you will always hear it from me. Does that sound fair?" Inmates respect people who are honest and strong enough not to be manipulated.

Be Objective—Don't Take Sides

Never interfere with a correctional officer in the performance of his or her duties. Never take sides in a dispute between an inmate and a correctional officer. If you have questions or comments about the way a situation was handled, discuss them with your supervisor in private. Follow the chain of command if you wish to lodge a complaint. If an inmate tries to get you involved, respond in a way that shows you respect the rules. For example: "That is between you and the officer." Encourage inmates to use the facility's grievance procedure if they feel an officer was wrong.

Sometimes inmates fear retaliation if they file a complaint against a correctional officer. On very rare occasions, I have helped facilitate a meeting between an inmate and a staff supervisor. In each case, I first discussed the complaint with my prison supervisor. This supervisor then decided how this complaint should be addressed and contacted the appropriate staff member. It is important for inmates to see that you will be supportive of them *and* that you will respect the chain of command.

Expect Hostility

Sooner or later, you will be faced with a hostile inmate. The inmate may be angry with you or with the whole world. When this happens volunteers should not try to force conversation. Listen to the inmate's grievances and give him or her a safe place to vent their feelings. Make sure you have a way to escape. Above all, do not act shocked or respond in a hostile, sarcastic, or anxious manner. Retain your composure and ignore the hostility or withdraw for awhile. Chances are the inmate will regain his or her composure in a few minutes.

47

Don't Expect to Be Thanked

Many inmates have never been taught how to say "thank you." Others find it embarrassing to show gratitude. As a result, volunteers may never hear those special words. Frequently, volunteers and staff members feel unappreciated and are tempted to quit. Every once in a while volunteers do get to see the fruit of their labor. This is what makes volunteering inside a correctional facility worthwhile. Unfortunately, most of the time volunteers must be satisfied with the knowledge that their work is appreciated—usually in ways that they will never know.

Suggestions and Rules

Although some prison rules may seem pointless, they are necessary to maintain discipline. A lot of them have been created as the results of unfortunate incidents. For example, many prisons won't let women bring in lipstick or wear wigs inside men's prisons. This is to keep inmates from escaping by being disguised as women.

Correctional facilities from across the country sent material to contribute to this book. The following helpful hints and regulations that would apply to most facilities were developed from that information:

1. Use appropriate language. Don't pick up inmate slang or vulgarity. Using language that isn't a part of your style can label you a phony. [*Arkansas*]

2. Do not volunteer if you are a relative or a visitor of an inmate in that institution. [*California*]

3. Do not engage in political activities during the time voluntary services are being performed. [*District of Columbia*]

4. Do not bring contraband into prison. If you are not sure what is contraband, ask the staff. People who bring in contraband are subject to permanent expulsion and/or arrest. [*Florida*]

5. Do not bring anything into or out of a facility for an inmate at any time, no matter how innocent or trivial it may seem, unless with the written permission of the superintendent. Volunteers should adopt a policy of

saying no to any request by an inmate to bring in cigarettes, money, magazines, or letters. If in doubt, ask a staff member. [*Pennsylvania*]

6. Keep everything in the open. Do not say or do anything with an inmate you would be embarrassed to share with your peers or supervisors. [*Kansas*]

7. Do not give up if you failed at your first try. Try again. [*Texas*]

8. Don't overidentify. Be a friend, but let inmates carry their own problems. Be supportive without becoming like the inmates in viewpoint or attitude. [*Minnesota*]

9. Do not take anything, including letters, in or out of a correctional facility without permission. Respect the confidentiality of records and other privileged information. [*Connecticut*]

10. Do not bring unauthorized visitors or guests with you to the institution. They will be refused admission. [*Maryland*]

11. Do not give out your address or telephone number. If asked, you might say, "I'm sorry, but I was told that it was against the rules to do that." [*Prison Fellowship*]

12. Do not correspond with inmates in the facility in which you volunteer or accept collect phone calls from them at your place of residence. [*New York*]

13. Be aware that the use of, or being under the influence of, alcohol or drugs while on institution grounds is prohibited. [*Ohio*]

14. Don't impose your values and beliefs on inmates. Do not let others impose a lower set of values on you. [*Oklahoma*]

15. Don't discuss the criminal justice system, the courts, inconsistency in sentencing, or related topics. Although everyone is entitled to his or her opinion, what volunteers say can have serious repercussions in the dorms or with staff. [*Wyoming*]

16. Ask for help. If you are uncertain about what to do or say, be honest. It is always best to tell the inmate that you will have to seek assistance from your supervisor. Inmates don't expect you to have all the answers. [*North Carolina*]

17. Know your personal and professional goals. Be firm, fair, and consistent. [*Washington*]

18. If you have done something inappropriate, tell your coordinator regardless of what happened. It is far better to be reprimanded than to become a criminal. [*Wisconsin*]

Dealing with Self-centered Inmates

As explained earlier, narcissism is the most prominent feature in the average inmate's personality. Self-centered people live by their own rules. This can make it difficult to lead groups in correctional settings.

Kiser (1987) describes the problems he had with inmates in a college-level class he was teaching. Several students refused to answer the roll. One refused to give his real name. Others wandered in and out of the classroom at will. Some stood in the hall for a while and simply stared into the classroom. Another refused to wait his turn while exams were returned and tried to pressure the professor into giving him his exam back first.

This story is not unusual. Inmates will do this and more just to demonstrate who actually has the power in the group. This means that instructors must decide how much of this type of behavior will be tolerated and take control of the group. Mallinger (1991) tells of an inmate who loudly announced, "I feel lousy today, so nobody better mess with me." Equally loud, Mallinger responded, "I feel like writing a misconduct report today, so nobody better mess with me." They parted amicably.

Rules must be explained and enforced with politeness, firmness, and consistency. This helps inmates learn that every action has consequences, some good and some bad. Through sensitive confrontation, inmates can be taught to demonstrate care and respect for others. Caring confrontation may also include asking or forcing unruly inmates to leave. Inmates often associate caring with weakness so to be effective, instructors must display "loving toughness."

Dealing with Inmates' External Locus of Control

As explained earlier, most inmates have an external locus of control. These inmates feel their lives are controlled by luck, the difficulty of the task, or powerful others. As a result, they feel grades or completion certificates are arbitrarily assigned by instructors.

The accompanying feeling of powerlessness can drain inmates' motivation to complete rehabilitation programs. Their attitude seems to be "it won't help, so why learn?" Others will do the minimum required to get their completion certificates or simply sit in class and not try.

This can be changed by showing inmates that they do have the power to complete rehabilitation programs. This requires programs to be designed with structured tasks that can be completed step-by-step. Program effectiveness will be increased if inmates know in advance *exactly* what they must do to successfully complete the program. They must *perceive* that these goals are within their grasp.

For example, in the family life psychoeducational programs I work with, inmates must meet three requirements to successfully complete the programs: (1) they must be on time and present during all the group sessions, (2) they must turn in all homework assignments, and (3) they must score at least 70 percent on the final exam. They understand that the rules are suspended only if prison staff require a change or for a genuine emergency. Breaks are given every hour so that going to the toilet or getting a drink of water is not considered an emergency. Inmates know that failure to comply with any of the requirements is actually a request not to be allowed to graduate. They also know that the instructor can be *trusted* to comply with their request.

There is a grace period of ten minutes (by the instructor's watch) at the beginning of each class. During that time, the material on the final exam is reviewed. Inmates are taught during the first session that the rules are supported by staff and designed to help them develop responsibility. It is emphasized that they will need this skill to get out of prison and stay out.

The first session begins with the question, "Who will determine if you will pass this course?" Invariably, the inmates will reply, "You." Four questions are then asked:

1. "Since the warden cleared your schedule, can you get here on time?"

2. "Can you turn in your homework?"

3. "Since the exam will be reviewed, can you study enough to make at least 70 percent?"

4. "Who will determine if you pass this course?"

The reply now becomes, "I will." Since I began starting the program with these questions, the average grade on the final exam has risen approximately ten points.

Inmates need to be taught that their success or failure will be determined by how well they fulfilled class requirements. Inmates who perceive they have the ability to successfully complete the requirements of programs will be the most successful.

Beating Inmates at Their Own Games

Creating and strictly enforcing the rules emphasize the link between behavior and its consequences. They also allow instructors to model ways of being in control while submitting to the external control of prison regulations, including using the chain of command, requesting that conflicting appointments be changed, submitting to security requirements, and working with staff members.

Language can be altered to confront criminal thinking patterns by introducing the concept of "earning" punishments. For example, instead of "What did the correctional officer give you for disobeying the order?" ask "What did you *earn* when you decided to disobey the correctional officer's order?" Statements such as "the judge *gave* me ten years" can be rephrased to "You mean you *earned* ten years the moment you committed the crime." To help them with their future, ask: "Once you are released on parole, what will you *earn* if you violate the conditions?" This can be followed with, "Isn't that like screaming 'Warden, I demand that you let me back in prison!'?"

Since most inmates don't have internal controls, external deterrents to crime must be stressed. These include fear of being caught, fear of injury, or fear of doing more time. Using internal deterrents such as "don't do crime so you won't have a guilty conscience" are probably ineffective. A better statement to use might be: "Don't do the crime if you can't do the time."

Even though correctional systems are controlling systems, effective volunteers show inmates how they can still have some control over their own destinies. Learning to be dependable and faithful can begin inside the prison walls. Pointing out how the inmate feels when he or she is the victim of narcissistic behavior is a good way to teach respect for the feelings of others.

Overcoming Inmate Resistance

In *Counseling the Involuntary and Resistant Client,* Harris and Watkins (1987) say that resistance is necessary to help people hang onto their identity. The most obvious forms include open hostility, silence, strained politeness, defensiveness, avoidance, and silliness. People display these behaviors for personal gain. Sometimes it's to overpower and get their own way. In other cases, the resistance is a reluctance to make suggested changes. In either case, inmates must see a reason to change before they will drop their resistance. Some resistance is caused by the inmate's inability to tolerate frustration. Change takes time. Inmates want an instant fix. They want what they want when they want it.

The use of metaphor is an effective way to overcome resistance. This could include a story that challenges their thinking patterns, a parable that teaches a value, a joke with an appropriate punch line, or images. An imaginary movie screen can help people see what their actions have cost them. The image of a bull in the china shop can help inmates overcome their use of anger as a means of resistance and/or control.

Frequently inmates will say, "You can't help me because you don't live here. You just don't know what it is like!" This can be countered with, "You're right, I don't know what it is like to live here. However, I do know how to live in the free world. Would you rather teach me how to live in here or learn how to live in the free world?"

"Forgetful" inmates may be asked, "What would happen if you began to remember and found out that you actually were guilty?" This allows them to save face and not appear to be a liar if they "suddenly" begin to remember at a later date.

Sometimes, inmates will remain resistant no matter how hard you try. Change is scary for most people. For criminals, giving up lifelong patterns means restructuring their entire world. Most won't apply the energy required to do this. But volunteers should keep trying; they may be planting a seed that will bear fruit later.

Theory of Change

The Cognitive Moral Theory for Changing Criminals, developed by Gupta and associates (Gupta 1988; Gupta & Mueller 1984) is based on the premise that people have as much capacity for doing good as for doing bad. Using this theory requires helping inmates through five stages. First, help inmates quit making excuses for their actions and accept responsibility for their own actions. Although alcohol, drugs, lack of love or too much love, and socioeconomic conditions are contributing factors, they do not cause people to commit crimes. Criminals do their crimes because they choose to do them and enjoy it.

Second, help them to become aware of the unfairness of the crime's effect on others. Teach them to see how much their crime has cost them and how much it has hurt their families. Teach them the aspects of the criminal personality and help them see how self-centered they really are.

Inmates have reached stage three when they start experiencing appropriate feelings of self-disgust and true guilt for the harm they have done. Stage four is using those feelings to motivate the inmate to make a commitment to change. Stage five is helping the inmate develop a plan to build a new and productive life.

Using Education to Produce Change

Mace (1981) claims that several steps must be taken before people change in response to education. First, the information must be given and the material understood. People must select the pieces of that newly learned knowledge that might apply to their own lives and experiment with the new concepts. Then, as they make commitments to use the new knowledge as a basis for growth, change can occur.

Helping Inmates with Their Religious Beliefs

Volunteers will frequently hear statements such as "I've turned my life over to God, and I know that He will keep me out once I'm released." This, of course, makes a "powerful other" responsible if the inmate fails.

Statements such as these can be countered with illustrations from the Bible. For example, Exodus 4 shows that God did not stop Moses from killing the Egyptian. Nor, as II Samuel 11 says, was David stopped from having an affair with Bathsheba and having her husband killed. These examples and others can be used to convince inmates that God allows individuals to follow their own desires. He also allows them to earn the consequences of their own decisions.

Many inmates use religion in a self-centered way. One inmate showed me a letter he was sending to his wife. In it he said: "We must follow God's teachings. We must get along like God says and be a happy couple." Like so many, he was unwilling to say that *he* would follow God's moral teachings and treat his wife with respect. Instead he wanted God to do the work and *make* his wife treat him with respect even when he was being self-centered.

Inmates need to understand that faith in God is not enough to create change. It takes a commitment to learn *and* follow the moral guidelines of the faith. Effective religious volunteers show them how to accomplish this task.

Helping Inmates to Heal Themselves

The following five concepts can help inmates end their criminal careers (Bayse 1991):

1. *Teach them how to love.* Show them that love is giving a part of yourself that is the best you have to offer, asking nothing in return except that the gifts be accepted. True gifts of love are never given for selfish reasons or personal gain. Rejecting gifts of love is rejecting the giver of the gift and not the gift itself. Accepting and exchanging gifts of love will cause

relationships to grow. Since love is something that you do and not something that you feel, anyone can start the loving process. It takes a strong person to show true love.

2. *Teach them how to forgive.* Forgiveness is not forgetting; we don't have the ability to do that. Forgiveness is a decision to treat the person like it never happened, while still holding them accountable for their actions. Accountability is to ensure that it doesn't happen again.

   Forgiving themselves requires that they admit their wrongs to the people involved and accept the consequences of their own behavior. They pay their debts to their family, their victims, and society by doing their time, changing their lifestyle, and making any needed restitution. Then, help them to accept the fact that they now have a clean slate. Show them how to stop punishing themselves and start living the rest of their lives as if their moral failures never happened. Inmates must understand that this is hard to do. It becomes especially hard when they face unforgiving people who constantly remind them of their failures.

3. *Give them the gift of self-esteem.* Self-esteem, and the feeling of completeness that follows, has four aspects: feeling loved, feeling accepted, feeling competent, and following ethical principles. Volunteers can help inmates develop self-esteem by giving or showing them how to develop these four aspects. Showing them respect and acceptance will fulfill the first two requirements. Helping them to develop areas of competence and teaching them how to practice ethical living will give them the ability to achieve the others.

4. *Teach them the keys to freedom.* It takes two keys to open the door to freedom. They are (*a*) respecting the rules of society and (*b*) taking responsibility for one's own actions. Teach them how to use these keys.

5. *Teach them to dream.* Everything we do starts with a dream that says: "I wonder what it would be like to *(fill in the blank)* ?" Help them to start dreaming about what it will be like to be a useful part of family life and society once released. Then, give them the tools to achieve that dream.

Healing Involves Pain

Pain is a very useful feeling. One of the worst things that can happen to someone is to lose the ability to feel pain. When this happens they can be hurt and not know it. Over the years, many inmates have killed their ability to feel emotional pain. Because of this, many have never had to accept responsibility for their own actions.

As inmates begin to realize how much grief they have caused others, their personal pain can become almost unbearable. They earned that pain, and a volunteer should not attempt to take it away. Instead, acknowledge their pain, but let them feel it. Help them realize that this pain is the consequence of their own actions. It's part of what they earned the moment they committed the crime. It is not something that someone else did to them. Surgery hurts, but the healing it produces makes it worth the pain.

Effective pain relief requires forgiveness and living a new lifestyle that doesn't cause more pain. Remembering the pain of past mistakes is an effective motivating tool.

Chapter 5

Avoiding the Pitfalls

Poor Judgment and Being Conned

Over the years, many have volunteered in correctional facilities with the hope of helping inmates. Some have left in shame. This chapter is designed to help volunteers recognize and avoid some of the common pitfalls facing correctional volunteers. Sometimes all it takes is one slip to start a landslide that can bury your reputation and freedom.

The 2 June 1992 issue of *The Montgomery Advertiser* carried a wire story about a criminal justice professor who was charged with helping two men break out of prison. He told police that he gave the inmates a cutting tool because he was in love with one of the inmates.

Unfortunately, cases like this happen all too frequently. Recently, a doctoral student who was serving his last month of internship on the mental health staff was arrested for trying to smuggle cocaine into prison. He said he felt sorry for the inmates.

Another volunteer was talked into mailing a letter addressed to an attorney for an inmate. Instead of legal papers, the envelope contained forged state identification cards made in the print shop. The "lawyer" was the inmate's brother. When the brothers were caught, the volunteer was accused of being the ringleader.

Mallinger (1991) tells of a librarian who was conned by an inmate who shared her love of poetry. He convinced her that it would be no big deal for her to smuggle some poetry books from his girlfriend into the prison. Unknown to the librarian, the books had drugs hidden in the bindings. When caught, the inmate eagerly told officials who brought the books to him. The librarian lost her job and was banned from ever working in another prison in that state.

In still another case, an inmate who had just arrived at the prison asked a volunteer to call a specific federal agent for him. He claimed to be finally ready to provide information about two high-ranking governmental officials' involvement in a drug smuggling operation. The volunteer made the call—without telling his prison or organization supervisor. The federal officer arrived unannounced. The story was false. The inmate's record showed that this same story was used in an attempted plea bargain. This volunteer ruined a twenty-year spotless record and was suspended for a year.

Arkansas' volunteer manual tells of an enthusiastic volunteer who, seeing the amount of work that needed to be done, gathered sixty sets of dentures that needed to be cleaned. In due time, this volunteer cleaned the dentures and proudly presented them to staff. Unfortunately, they were all mixed up in a wash basin! The task of returning the dentures took weeks because many of the inmates were convinced that theirs did not fit as well as before.

We all make mistakes, and volunteers make enough to fill a book. Fortunately most are not as serious as the ones reported here. However, having to correct blunders creates a lot of tension and resistance to volunteers from staff members. Becoming part of the team can help keep mistakes like these from happening.

Problem Areas

On occasion, there is an uneasy truce between many volunteers and prison staff. The Joint Commission on Correctional Manpower and Training found that volunteers tended to be overconfident and insensitive to the problems inherent to a correctional facility. Because of this, some volunteers do more harm than good.

Some create problems by becoming angry with the system. Effective volunteers understand that the need for security overrides any other need in a correctional facility. Still, some protest loudly if searched. This makes officers look even harder because they know that the people who howl the loudest frequently have the most to hide. Some Alcoholics or Narcotics Anonymous volunteers dislike revealing their full names for security checks, signing in, or identification badges because it violates the organization's principle of confidentiality among members. Helping inmates starts by modeling willing compliance with security requirements.

Many volunteers have an inflated view of the good they can accomplish. This can cause problems. Volunteers come, spend their few hours, and go home. Many see inmates make *apparent* changes and get excited. Others, who do not see the expected results, become discouraged quickly. These people have fallen into the "instant success" trap. Change occurs slowly. Volunteers who see "instantaneous" change are usually reaping the harvest of previous work done by other team workers. The ones who don't see any apparent changes may have planted seeds that will bear fruit later.

Many volunteers become angry if correctional officers display negative attitudes. This sort of problem should be handled through the chain of command. Officers *are* in charge of their space, and only *their* supervisors can override their orders. If you are having problems with an officer, make sure you're not the source. Over the years many volunteers have presented a superior attitude and looked down on correctional officers. Others, anxious to be the "good guy," help inmates perpetuate the idea that staff members are the "bad guys." These attitudes are not the way to gain the cooperation of security staff.

Being gullible can cause big problems. Many inmates can tell the biggest lies with the straightest face. Take everything you hear with a grain of salt. Horror stories of assaults, strip searches, homosexuality, drugs, and abuses by officers abound. Some are true. Most aren't. Inmates, like many people, thrive on rumors, allegations, and gossip. The stories are designed to win your sympathy.

Volunteers will see and hear many things in prison that they don't understand. When this happens, they should talk to their supervisors or the supervisor on duty before taking action. Know and use the chain of command. Don't do like two volunteer worship leaders did following an evening service. After listening to an inmate describe how he was refused his medicine and feared death, they left the institution in a huff without going to the supervisor first. A few minutes later they were banging on the door to the warden's house. The warden quickly accompanied the angry volunteers back to the prison and discovered that the story was false. The two volunteers are no longer welcome at that prison.

Many religious volunteers complain that chaplains "aren't spiritual enough." Indeed, some *are* better than others. Most ministers only see their people on Sundays. Chaplains spend forty hours a week or more with inmates who are self-centered, manipulative, and use religion to meet their own needs. Many volunteers have preconceived ideas about the needs of inmates but little experience or training to back their ideas. Good help and funding are hard to find. Instead of criticizing, try praying for these chaplains. Ask God to show you, and the chaplain, ways to minister to the inmates. Respect their authority and encourage them. Help them feed their flock instead of planting seeds of discord. This may even produce the spiritual awakening that you may desire.

Many problems correctional facilities have with volunteers could be solved if the volunteers would model the keys to freedom: respecting the rules of the system and taking responsibility for their own actions. This includes using the prison's and, if applicable, the volunteer organization's chain of command.

How Volunteers Get Conned

The word "con" can be defined as smooth talk used to extract a violation of regulations. It works. Sometimes volunteers are tempted to say, "They don't follow the rules, so why should we?" If you ever find yourself becoming willing to bend a rule to help an inmate, you have just become a prime target for the con game.

The methods used are limited only by the inmate's imagination. However, Washington's *Volunteer Manual* lists some of the more common strategies:

1. The inmate engages in long conversations about the volunteer's likes, dislikes, or other personal matters.

2. The inmate suddenly offers favors, does extra work, and is excessively nice and complimentary.

3. The inmate begins to ask for materials in excess of what is allowed by policy.

4. The inmate will not take no for an answer.

5. The inmate defies orders and/or breaks minor rules.

6. The inmate tries to turn staff members and/or volunteers against each other.

7. The inmate tries to get his or her way by instilling fear.

8. The inmate pushes the staff or volunteers to the limits of their patience hoping to get his or her way.

Don't automatically assume that because an inmate is nice that he or she is trying something. Not all inmates are manipulative. Some genuinely desire nothing more than a close working relationship with someone who cares. Nonmanipulative inmates will not be offended if they are told, "I'm sorry, but that's against the rules," or "I'm not sure, let me check with my supervisor." One of the best ways to keep from being manipulated is to never do or say anything you would not want to be made public.

Games Inmates Play

The following are six scenes volunteers commonly face dramatized in the National Institute of Corrections training video *Volunteer and Contract Service Employees*. They are all variations of the inmate con game.

"Just a Touch"

A female English teacher and a male inmate are talking after class. After a period of small talk and flattery, the inmate expresses concern about newly developing homosexual urges. "It's been three years," he explains, "can I touch you just once to reassure myself that I'm still a man?"

Ethical standards require volunteers and staff to maintain a professional distance from inmates. This is the only way to remain objective and focused on their needs. Should you discover that a relationship is building between you and an inmate, or if an inmate "comes on" to you, report it to your supervisor. Doing so can protect you later if the inmate tries to use it against you. If you wish to continue with the relationship, be prepared to quit doing volunteer work at that prison. You could then apply to be on that inmate's visitor list.

Romantic attraction and sexual involvement between volunteers and inmates is a major problem in prison systems. Many inmates see any sign of caring as a sexual signal. Some inmates desire the relationship for the power it produces. Volunteers who enjoy the flattery forget that most affairs start with "innocent" flirtation. "Forbidden fruit" usually ruins the lives of those who try it.

"Save Me from the Demon"

An inmate asks the volunteer drug treatment counselor to help him with plans for his imminent release. Fearing relapse, the inmate begs the counselor to accept him as one of his clients and rent him the room that is available at his house. "Just give me your name and address and my brother will bring you the money to hold the room."

This is a common theme: "You're the only one who can help me." This theme includes requests to call wives, family members, or judges on their behalf. Although this is flattering, volunteers must be careful to maintain a professional distance from inmates. Instead, help them learn how to use the resources available to help themselves. Externally focused inmates frequently turn on volunteers and blame them if the proposed intervention does not work.

Volunteers should be careful of the information they provide inmates. For example, volunteers should never give out their home phone numbers or addresses to inmates. It is not unusual for inmates to harass, beg assistance, threaten, or even harm trusting volunteers. If volunteers feel they have a legitimate reason for doing follow-up work once released, it should be cleared with their supervisor before being offered.

"Easy for You, Sister"

A volunteer instructor is talking to an inmate who has done well in previous classes. Now the student has stopped trying. Instead of accepting the instructor's challenge to use her talents, the inmate explodes, "It's easy for you to say, sister! You got your fancy job, your fine college degree, and doing your civic duty volunteering in this joint." With that the inmate angrily runs out of the classroom.

Even though it is painful to watch, good instructors allow students to reap the failure they earn if they stop doing the work. It is not unusual for 50 percent of the students in a correctional setting to simply quit. The average inmate has a low frustration tolerance. Even though they may have the ability, many do not have the staying power to complete assignments. When this happens, externally focused inmates will blame the volunteer for their failure.

It is important for volunteers to understand inmate personality and provide continual encouragement. As a volunteer instructor, I pair students so that the academically strong can help the weak. I also provide tutoring to any inmate who requests it, and I review the exam content in class. In spite of all this, some inmates will simply sit in class, not try, then become angry because I won't "give" them their diploma.

It is very important for volunteers in a correctional setting to show that they can't be manipulated into bending the rules. To avoid burnout, volunteers should focus on inmates who do change and allow the others to reap the consequences of their own actions.

"They're out to Get Us"

Inmates tell the volunteer that two correctional officers are beating inmates for "kicks"—with the captain's permission. They claim to be unable to mail a letter to their attorney because the prison censors their mail. The scene ends with an inmate saying, "All I'm asking you to do is mail one lousy letter."

This is a typical con game. The common goal is to get the volunteer to break a rule that would benefit the inmate. Many inmates have become experts at telling stories that would pull on anyone's heartstrings. Some volunteers become callous and simply refuse the requests.

However, there is a slight chance that the story could be true. Unfortunately, cases of brutality do occasionally happen in prison. As such, these charges can't be ignored. In this case, since a captain was accused, the volunteer could offer to check with his supervisor and arrange a meeting with the warden. He would find out quickly if the inmates were serious. If not, the inmates would say things like, "The warden don't care about us so why bother?"

Variations of the same con game are asking volunteers to make phone calls or bring packages from their "families" into or out of the facility. Volunteers may protect themselves from being conned by saying, "Let me ask my supervisor to see if it will be all right to do what you have asked."

Being asked to write a letter of reference is not part of the con game. This is a common request of a volunteer instructor. If you feel that this would be appropriate, clear it with your supervisor first. A copy of the letter of reference should also be placed in the inmate's file.

"Not on the List"

An inmate is present who is not on the approved attendance list. The inmate claims staff forgot to include his name.

This does happen sometimes. Inmates are also known to attend functions to get out of their assignments. Volunteers would be within their rights to ask the inmate to leave. Another response might be, "Let me check with my supervisor and see if it would be all right for you to stay."

"The Fight"

Two inmates start a fight in the classroom. The volunteer instructor panics, tries to get an inmate to stop it, runs past the telephone, and out of the room. As soon as she leaves, an inmate steals some items from her purse, which she left on the desk. She returns and calls for help.

If an inmate gets hostile, you should talk calmly and avoid being argumentative. Signal a staff person. If alone, maneuver yourself into the vision or hearing range of a staff member. If you have one, blow a whistle. Do not attempt to resolve the situation on your own, get assistance from staff—correctional officers are trained to handle such situations.

It is important to remember that every inmate in prison has been convicted of a felony offense. Prisons and jails are harsh places. Many inmates have spent their entire lives forcing their will on others through physical violence. Occasionally, they become angry enough to attack staff members and volunteers. If this happens, use the system. Require that the inmate face the consequences of his or her behavior by filing the appropriate disciplinary or criminal charges.

What about Riots?

Prison riots do happen occasionally. When they do, they make headlines across the nation. However, as Maryland's volunteer training material says, "the chance of being taken hostage is probably as remote as the possibility of being struck down by lightning." If a riot should occur, volunteers should remember that prison staff have received extensive training to respond to this event. Most riots end in less than five hours—without injury.

Planning for the unexpected can prevent catastrophe. Washington's *Volunteer Handbook* provides several suggestions for volunteers who find themselves held captive:

1. Don't act foolishly; heroics can get you hurt.

2. Be cooperative and comply with the captor's demands.

3. Look for a place to take cover, such as under a desk, in case authorities or inmates attempt to storm your area.

4. Keep a low profile, and avoid the appearance of observing crimes rioters commit.

5. Do not make threats or attempt to negotiate with captors.

6. Try to act natural and listen if the captors want to talk.

7. Be observant and write down your observations as soon as you are released.

8. Seek counseling when it's over. Some things in life are not meant to be handled alone.

Keep Good Records

Keep accurate records of what you do inside a correctional facility. This should include the days worked, number of hours worked, and activities performed while there. Some states allow this time to count toward experience requirements for civil service employment. Your volunteer coordinator should know if this would apply to you.

In some cases, travel and other expenses for volunteer work can be deducted from your state and federal taxes. Consult your tax advisor to see if you would be eligible for this deduction.

Make Sure You're Covered

It is extremely rare for an inmate to file a lawsuit against a volunteer; however, it does happen. Some states now have laws protecting volunteers from lawsuits. Some states provide liability insurance that covers approved volunteers while they are working inside a correctional facility. Others provide worker's compensation insurance that pays to have injuries treated. Groups may provide coverage for their volunteers. Individuals may be covered by their homeowner's policy. Ask the appropriate person if you're covered. Volunteers should know whether they are covered before giving their time to any organization.

Organizations of Interest

The **American Correctional Association (4380 Forbes Blvd., Lanham, MD 20706-4322)** is a multidisciplinary organization consisting of correctional professionals, individuals, agencies, and organizations involved in the entire spectrum of correctional activities. Joining this organization can help you stay abreast of the ever-changing world of correctional service. Reasonably priced memberships are available to volunteers and professionals alike; benefits include a subscription to the magazine *Corrections Today* and discounts on books published by ACA. For information, call 800-ACA-JOIN.

The **American Jail Association** (1000 Day Road, Suite 100, Hagerstown, MD 21740) is a professional organization dedicated to the improvement of the nation's jails. It produces a magazine, books, and videotapes covering a wide variety of jail training topics. For information, call 301-790-3930.

The **International Association of Addiction and Offender Counselors** is part of the American Counseling Association (5999 Stevenson Avenue, Alexandria, VA 22304). Membership is limited to professionals in the counseling or human development fields. Membership benefits include professional journal subscriptions, the availability of professional liability insurance, and a monthly newsletter. For information, call 800-347-6647.

The **Family and Corrections Network** (P.O. Box 59, Batesville, VA 22924) is a national, professional organization that works to reduce crime by strengthening family ties. It shares skills and resources with people who provide programs and services for the families of inmates.

The **National Institute of Corrections Information Center** (1860 Industrial Circle, Suite A, Longmont, CO 80503) has a library of information available for use. For information, call 303-682-0213.

The **Federal Bureau of Prisons** (BOP) has a newsletter,

Volunteer Today, that is for and about volunteers. To be placed on the mailing list, contact the volunteer coordinator at any BOP correctional facility or write to the Office of Citizen Participation, Federal Bureau of Prisons, 320 First St., N.W., Washington, DC 20534.

Avoid Burnout

Frequently, volunteers feel like failures when one of "their" inmates returns to prison after being released. This happens, and when it does, volunteers should remind themselves that inmates chose to do the act that earned them more time. Volunteers should focus on the inmates who do change.

Volunteers usually give of their time because they care. There simply aren't enough hours in the day to fill all of the needs. It is important to enter a correctional facility with clear guidelines of what you can realistically expect to accomplish in the time allowed. Judging yourself on this criterion will allow you to feel a sense of accomplishment and can help keep you from burning out.

Volunteer work with inmates is not easy. Many times you will want to throw up your arms and quit. I find this happening when I look at the large number of inmates who refuse to change instead of the small number who actually do change. Success in correctional rehabilitation is measured one inmate at a time. Each one who is rehabilitated and becomes a useful member of society is no longer a criminal. Who can put a price on one changed life? That's why we choose to volunteer.

Glossary of Prison Slang

In the early 1970s, I was called to a Virginia maximum security prison to investigate an attempted murder of one inmate by another. Right out of the academy, I was a "gung-ho" rookie trooper on his first case inside the prison. The primary suspect was an inmate serving life without parole for committing several murders. This big, burly, rough-talking man was the self-appointed "godfather" of the prison yard.

During questioning, the inmate became belligerent and threatened me. To show that I wasn't afraid, I looked him straight in the eye and said, "Listen, punk!" The inmate wanted to kill me and probably would have if the correctional officers had not forcibly carried him back to his cell—screaming threats all the way. I didn't find out until later why I had almost caused a riot.

This glossary is included so that you won't make the same kinds of mistakes that I did. My first was using slang. Don't expect to be treated like a professional if you don't sound like one. My second was not knowing that inmates frequently assign different meanings to words than we do. For example, the word "inmate" means something entirely different than "convict."

This glossary was compiled from lists provided by inmates and prison systems from across the country. These definitions are not absolute—prison slang changes frequently.

Baby raper: Child molester
Blood: Inmate of the same race
Boss: (1) Supervisor, (2) term used in the southern United States for a correctional officer
Bounce: Try something (e.g., Bounce it off the volunteers and see if they'll go along with it.)
Box breaker: An inmate who steals from another inmate's locker
Brass: Prison or jail supervisors
Bug juice: (1) Artificially flavored, sweetened noncarbonated drink, (2) medicine

Bust your heart: A threat to kill

Buzzard: Someone who waits for a person to be raped by someone else before attempting to get sex from the victim

Candy man: Child molester

Case: A court charge (e.g., I was doing okay until I caught this case.)

Cludge: Gang up on someone and beat him or her up

Coke: (1) any form of soft drink, (2) slang for cocaine

Convict: (1) Technically, an inmate, (2) slang for a hardened criminal, one who demonstrates little evidence of abandoning his/her criminal thinking patterns, lives by the inmate code

Cop a plea: Plea bargain, admit to a lesser charge

Cop talk: How inmates dismiss anything that suggests that they should live by the rules of society (e.g., That's just cop talk.)

Do-rag: Bandana that shows gang affiliation

Doing a pound: A five-year sentence

Dope: (1) Drugs (e.g., You got any dope?), (2) information (e.g., Did you get the dope you needed to file your appeal?)

Drop a dime (quarter): (1) Inform on someone, being a snitch (e.g., He'll drop a dime in a heartbeat.), (2) make a phone call

Duck head: Crazy person, senseless

EOS: End of sentence

Easy prey: A gullible person

Fall: Deliberately accepting the fault for something someone else did (e.g., I took a fall for my friend.)

Fall partner: Partner in crime

Free world: Life on the outside, anything other than prison

Fresh meat: A new inmate arriving at the prison, especially a young first offender

F--k boy: A male willing to take the passive role in homosexual sex

Gunning one down: Masturbating to a female correctional officer

Gunslinger: Masturbator

Hack: Correctional officer (see Screw)

Hit: (1) A dose of drugs, (2) to play on, ask for (e.g., I hit on him for some cigarettes.)

Homeboy, homie, honcho: Inmate from your hometown

Hooch juice: Homemade prison booze or smuggled-in liquor

Hot-rail: (1) Term used by inmates to inform fellow inmates that a correctional officer is coming, (2) a lookout who watches for security

Hustle: (1) being taken advantage of (e.g., See if you can hustle the volunteers out of their cigarettes.), (2) the way you make money out of the hobby-crafts

Ink slinger: Tattoo artist

Inmate: (1) Technically, someone who has been convicted of a crime and is housed in a correctional facility, (2) slang for a temporary resident of the facility; inmates show signs of rehabilitation and/or a desire to learn how to abandon their criminal thinking patterns and learn from their mistakes *(see Convict)*

Inmate code: See nothing, say nothing, know nothing

Instant biker: Someone who has a Harley Davidson tattoo, but knows nothing about motorcycles

Jailhouse Jesus: Claims to be a Christian but doesn't act like one

Joint: (1) Jail, prison, (2) marijuana cigarette

Jones: A habit you can't break (e.g., I've got a jones for drugs and cigarettes.)

Jonesing: Coming down off a high and having no more drugs to create another high

Jumping the fence: (1) an escape, (2) leaving the convict role and becoming an inmate

Kick the bo-bo: Idle, meaningless talk

Kite: (1) Unauthorized or illegal letter, (2) a note (e.g., If you want to see the classification officer, send up a kite.)

Lever: Something that can be used against you

Lockdown: All inmates are confined to their cells; no inmate movement

Monkey on my back: A strong craving for alcohol or other drugs

Mule: Employee or volunteer who brings in contraband for inmates

Mule skinner: Homosexual male

On the streets: Outside of prison

Package: Nickname for contraband (e.g., Did you bring my package?)

Patsy: One who allows himself or herself to be used by others

Pearl handle: Brand-name, commercially prepared filtered cigarettes

Police: Anyone in authority, especially correctional officers

Pull his coat: Warn an inmate

Punk: A male who is willing to take the "female" or passive role in homosexual activity; being called a punk (or any other word symbolizing this) is considered *highly* offensive and has started many fights in prison systems *(see F--k boy, Sissy, or Queen)*

Queen: A male who is willing to take the passive role in homosexual activity

Rap: (1) Talk, (2) conviction of a crime (e.g., took the rap)

71

Rap partner: Someone to talk with

Reefer: Marijuana

Screws: Correctional officers

Send you home to your mother: A death threat

Shakedown: Search an area in the facility without warning

Shank: Homemade knife or spear-like weapon

Shark: Inmate who loans to others for personal gain

Sissy: Homosexual male *(see Punk)*

Slick legging: Going through the motions of intercourse without removing the clothing

Snitch: Tattletale

Snow man: Drug dealer—this may refer to someone who is willing to bring drugs into the prison or jail for inmates

Snuff out: To kill

Square: A cigarette

Stand-up dude: Dependable person

Stash: Inmate's personal storage of excessive amounts of any item, including drugs, cigarettes, soap, and toothpaste (e.g., How many cigarettes have you got in your stash?)

Store: (1) Prison commissary where personal items may be purchased, (2) the amount of money the inmate has in his or her personal account, (3) an illegal private enterprise where one inmate sells contraband goods to others at inflated prices

Stretch: Prison time served (e.g., She had a ten-year stretch.)

Sugar: (1) Homosexual, (2) someone special

Take it to the box: Jury trial

Ticket: Being written up for a violation of prison rules

Tight: Having a close personal relationship (e.g., That inmate and volunteer are tight.)

Tree jumper: (1) A rapist, (2) child molester

Wasted: (1) Killed, (2) dead drunk (e.g., I got wasted before I did my crime.)

Weed: Marijuana

Zip: Zero, nothing (e.g., He didn't get zip.)

Bibliography

American Correctional Association. 1978. *A handbook for volunteers in corrections.* College Park, Md.: American Correctional Association.

American Psychiatric Association. 1987. *Diagnostic and statistical manual of mental disorders.* 3d edition, revised. Washington, D.C.: American Psychiatric Association.

Andrews, W. 1970. *Old-time punishments.* Detroit, Mich.: Singing Tree Press.

Arkansas Department of Correction. n.d. *Volunteer manual.* Pine Bluff, Ark.: Arkansas DOC.

Barnes, H. E. 1972. *The story of punishment: A record of man's inhumanity to man.* 2d edition. Montclair, N.J.: Patterson Smith.

Bayse, D. J. 1989. *A study of the effect of family life education on prisoners' narcissism, locus of control, and view of ideal family functioning.*: Unpublished master's thesis, Auburn University, Auburn, Ala.

Bayse, D. J. 1991. *As free as an eagle: The inmate's family survival guide.* Laurel, Md.: American Correctional Association.

Bayse, D. J., S. M. Allgood, and P. H. Van Wyk. 1991. Family life education: An effective tool for prisoner rehabilitation. *Family Relations* 40:254-57.

Bayse, D. J., S. M. Allgood, and P. C. Van Wyk. 1992. Locus of control, narcissism, and family life education in correctional rehabilitation. *The Journal of Offender Rehabilitation* 17 (3/4): 47-64.

Buckley, M. 1974. *Breaking into prison: A citizen guide to volunteer action.* Boston, Mass.: Beacon Press.

Cesarez, G., and J. Madrid-Bustos. 1991. Taking a multicultural world view in today's corrections facilities. *Corrections Today* 53 (7): 68-71.

Colson, C., and D. Van Ness. 1989. *Convicted: New hope for ending America's crime crisis.* Westchester, Ill.: Crossway Books.

Connecticut Department of Correction. n.d. *Volunteer handbook.* Hartford, Conn.: Connecticut DOC.

Criminal Justice Institute. 1990. *The corrections yearbook: Instant answers to key questions in corrections.* Salem, N.Y.: Criminal Justice Institute.

Czudner, G. 1985. Changing the criminal: A theoretical proposal for change. *Federal Probation* 49 (3): 64-66.

Czudner, G., et al. 1984. *The 15 characteristics of the criminal.* Guelph, Ontario: Guelph Correctional Centre Psychology Department. Unpublished manuscript.

Day, S. J. 1992. *Religious service program volunteer pre-service guide.* Baltimore, Md.: State of Maryland Division of Correction, Religion Service Program. Unpublished manuscript.

Dobson, J. 1980. *Emotions: Can you trust them?* New York: Bantam Books.

Earle, A. M. 1896. *Curious punishment of bygone days.* Chicago, Ill.: Herbert S. Stone & Co.

Ganley, A. L. 1991. Perpetrators of domestic violence: An overview of counseling the court-mandated client. In *Tough customers: Counseling unwilling clients,* ed. G. A. Harris. Laurel, Md.: American Correctional Association.

Gartner, J., et al. 1990. *Final report on year one: Prison Fellowship research project.* Washington, D.C.: Prison Fellowship Ministries. Unpublished research project internal report prepared by the Institute for Religious Research, Loyola College in Maryland.

Glicken, V. K., and M. D. Glicken. 1982. The utilization of locus of control theory in treatment. *The Indian Journal of Social Work* 2:173-85.

Greenfeld, L. A. 1992. *Prisons and prisoners in the United States.* Washington, D.C.: U.S. Department of Justice.

Griffith, J. 1984. Evidence of unidimensionality of locus of control in women prisoners: Implications for prisoner rehabilitation. *Journal of Offender Counseling, Services and Rehabilitation* 9 (1/2): 57-69.

Gupta, P. K. 1988. *Case management in corrections.* Guelph, Ontario: Guelph Correctional Centre.

Gupta, P. K., and R. Mueller. 1984. The correction of criminal thinking and behavior through the cognitive-moral approach. *Correctional Options* 4:27-29.

Harris, G. A., ed. 1991. *Tough customers: Counseling unwilling clients.* Laurel, Md.: American Correctional Association.

Harris, G. A., and D. Watkins. 1987. *Counseling the involuntary and resistant client.* Laurel, Md.: American Correctional Association.

Harris, Louis and Associates. 1969. *Volunteers look at corrections.* Washington, D.C.: Joint Commission on Correctional Manpower and Training.

Heider, F. 1958. *The psychology of interpersonal relations.* New York: John Wiley and Sons.

Hibbert, C. 1978. *The roots of evil: A social history of crime and punishment.* Westport, Conn.: Greenwood Press.

Jankowski, L. W. 1992. *Correctional population in the United States, 1990.* Washington, D.C.: U.S. Department of Justice.

Kiser, G. C. 1987. Disciplinary problems among inmate college students. *Federal Probation* 51 (3): 42-48.

Lambert, J. 1991. Training staff to take a new approach to today's diverse inmate population. *Corrections Today* 53 (7): 168-71.

MacDonald, A. P., Jr. 1971. Internal-external locus of control: Parental antecedents. *Journal of Consulting and Clinical Psychology* 37 (1): 141-47.

Mace, D. 1981. The long, long train from information-giving to behavioral change. *Family Relations* 30:599-606.

Mallinger, S. 1991. Games inmates play. *Corrections Today* 53 (December): 188-92.

Maryland Department of Public Safety and Correctional Services. 1989. *Operation manual for Maryland Division of Correction volunteers.* Baltimore: Maryland Division of Correction.

The Montgomery Advertiser. Professor says he helped in escape of lover inmate. 2 June 1992, 3a.

National Institute of Corrections. 1984. *Volunteer and contract service employees.* Boulder, Colo.: NIC. Videotape.

National Institute of Corrections. 1984. *Volunteer and contract service employee training instructor's manual.* Boulder, Colo.: NIC.

New Mexico Corrections Department. n.d. *A handbook for volunteers in corrections in New Mexico.* Santa Fe, N.M.: New Mexico Corrections Department.

New York Department of Correctional Services. n.d. *Guidelines for volunteer services.* Albany, N.Y.: New York Department of Correctional Services.

North Carolina Department of Correction. 1991. *Volunteers make a difference.* Raleigh, N.C.: North Carolina DOC Division of Prisons.

North Carolina Department of Correction. 1992. *Handbook for Volunteer Coordinator.* Raleigh, N.C.: North Carolina DOC Division of Prisons.

Offender/victim Ministries. 1990. *M-2 sponsor's handbook.* Newton, Kan.: Offender/victim Ministries.

Oklahoma Department of Corrections. n.d. *Handbook for citizen involvement in corrections.* Oklahoma City: Oklahoma DOC.

Prison Fellowship Ministries. 1989. *Prison Fellowship volunteer training volunteer's manual: Opening the door.* Washington, D.C.: Prison Fellowship Ministries.

Riggs, C., and S. van Baalen. 1992. The pastoral needs of women in prison. In *Female offenders: Meeting needs of a neglected population.* Laurel, Md.: American Correctional Association.

Romig, C. A., and C. Gruenke. 1991. The use of metaphor to overcome inmate resistance to mental health counseling. *Journal of Counseling and Development* 69 (5): 414-18.

Rotter, J. B. 1975. Some problems and misconceptions related to the construct of internal versus external control of reinforcement. *Journal of Consulting and Clinical Psychology* 43:56-67.

Salter, A. C. 1988. *Treating child sex offenders and victims: A practical guide.* Newbury Park, Calif.: Sage.

Samenow, S. E. 1984. *Inside the criminal mind.* New York: Times Books.

Schmalleger, F. 1986. *A history of corrections: Emerging ideologies and practices.* Bristol, Ind.: Wyndham Hall Press.

State of California. 1991. *Barclays official California code of regulations: Division 3 Department of Corrections.* San Francisco: Barclays Law Publishers.Sue, D. W., and D. Sue. 1990. *Counseling the culturally different.* New York: John Wiley & Sons.

Sykes, G., and S. L. Messinger. *The inmate social code.* Topeka, Kan.: Kansas DOC. Unpublished paper.

U.S. Department of Justice. 1988. *Report to the nation on crime and justice,* 2d edition. Washington, D.C.: U.S. Government Printing Office.

U.S. Department of Justice. 1990. *Sourcebook of criminal justice statistics—1989.* Washington, D.C.: U.S. Government Printing Office.

U.S. Department of Justice. 1991. *Drugs and crime facts, 1990.* Washington, D.C.: U.S. Department of Justice.

U.S. Department of Justice. August 1991. *Drugs and jail inmates, 1989.* Washington, D.C.: U.S. Department of Justice.

U.S. Department of Justice. 1992. *Bureau of Justice Statistics national update* 2, no. 1. Washington, D.C.: U.S. Department of Justice.

U.S. Department of Justice. March 1992. *Women in jail 1989.* Washington, D.C.: U.S. Department of Justice.

U.S. Department of Justice. May 1992. *Prisoners in 1991.* Washington, D.C.: U.S. Department of Justice.

U.S. Department of Justice. June 1992. *Jail inmates 1991.* Washington, D.C.: U.S. Department of Justice.

Wallbank, T. W., et al. 1978. *Civilization past and present.* 5th edition. Glenview, Ill.: Scott, Foresman and Company.

Washington State Department of Corrections. n.d. *Community involvement program volunteer handbook.* Olympia, Wash.: Washington State DOC.

Whitney, J. 1936. *Elizabeth Fry: Quaker heroine.* Boston, Mass.: Little, Brown, and Co.

Whittaker, R. 1990. Manning a women's prison—One officer's viewpoint. *Corrections Today* 52 (7): 158.

Wisconsin Department of Corrections. 1992. *Dodge Correctional Institution volunteer handbook.* Wauppun, Wis.: Wisconsin DOC.

Wyoming Women's Center. n.d. *Wyoming visitor's center visitor's guide.* Lusk, Wy.: Wyoming Women's Center.

Yochelson, S., and S. E. Samenow. 1976. A profile for change. *The criminal personality* 1. New York: Jason Aronson.

Yochelson, S., and S. E. Samenow. 1977. The change process. *The criminal personality* 2. New York: Jason Aronson.

Yochelson, S., and S. E. Samenow. 1986. The change process. *The criminal personality* 3. Northvale, N.J.: Jason Aronson.

About the Author

Daniel Justin Bayse served for seven years in the U.S. Navy, followed by ten years as a member of the Virginia State Police. He is the founder and executive director of Prison Family Foundation, Inc.

In August 1983, he entered Florida Baptist Theological College in Graceville, Florida, and received a bachelor of theology degree in December 1986. He received a master of science degree in family and child development from Auburn University in August 1989 and a specialist in education degree in community agency counseling in August 1992.

Bayse was ordained in 1987 by the First Baptist Church, Dothan, Alabama, and has specialized in family and prison ministry since 1983. Since 1988, as a minister, Bayse has provided more than 4,000 hours of volunteer service to the Alabama Department of Corrections and other prison systems. During this time, he wrote, implemented, and researched Alabama's first three family life education programs for inmates and their families. To date, more than 1,200 inmates and their families have been through one or more of these programs.

He was named a certified family life educator by the National Council on Family Relations in 1988 and received second place in their 1989 national "student of the year" competition for his work with inmates. He was included in the 1989 edition of *Who's Who in American Christian Leadership*.

Bayse is a member of the American Correctional Association, the National Council on Family Relations, the Family and Corrections Network, the American Counselors Association, the International Association of Addictions and Offender Counselors, and the International Association of Marriage and Family Counselors.

He is the author of the nation's first comprehensive self-help book for inmates and their families. *As Free As An Eagle: The Inmate's Family Survival Guide* was published in 1991 by the American Correctional Association.